A Wizard's Guide to Study Skills

Middle School Edition

Irene J. Hartzell, Ph.D.

Kids Like Learning, LLC

A **WIZARDS GUIDES**® Publication

Editor and illustrator — Thomas Butler

Book design — Raye Daniels

Author photo — Meryl Alcabes Photography

Printed in the United States of America

ISBN 978-0- 9984001-1-2

In memory of my dear friend and mentor, John I. Arena,

Founder of Academic Therapy Publications

and a True Wizard!

ACKNOWLEDGMENTS

I'm very grateful to so many people who aided in the creation of this special book for middle school students. Without their enthusiastic support **A Wizard's Guide** would still only be a dream.

I am most grateful to Tom Butler, editor and illustrator, for his enthusiasm, ingenuity and contributions.

Thanks go also to Raye Daniels for providing the excellent book design and formatting for publication.

Without the friendship and creative wisdom of my dear friend John Arena I would never have been inspired to write this book. His son, Jim Arena and widow Anne have given their unwavering support of this project. Under Jim's leadership Academic Therapy Publications has a major role in providing educational therapy materials for students throughout our country. Their steadfast friendship over the years helped make this book a reality.

In particular, I want to thank the middle school students who volunteered their time and effort to read the book and provide worthwhile feedback. Whenever possible, their ideas and suggestions were incorporated into improving the book.

Thanks go also to Prof. Robert A. Bjork, UCLA Distinguished Research Professor in the Dept. of Psychology, Director of the Learning and Forgetting Laboratory. Prof. Bjork's research served as a guiding beacon in the development of this book.

My family and many friends not only provided encouragement but also many useful suggestions along the way. I cannot name you all here - the list is very long - but you know who you are and **I appreciate all your ideas and your caring so much!**

A Wizard's Guide to Study Skills is designed to help Middle School students acquire the tools needed to meet the increasing academic challenge of High School.

Middle School is critical, it's the transition between one style of learning and another. It prepares you for the more rigorous requirements of High School.

This **Guide** represents an innovative knowledge centered approach based on research findings about human learning.

Scientists (**Wizards**) have studied human learning for a long time with the goal of improving how we learn. Some of their ideas may seem simple, but they're based on recent discoveries about how the brain works. Now we're putting together what researchers have learned so students can take advantage of this new information.

As we move ahead in the book you'll learn many things. You'll gain insights and acquire practical tools to help you study better.

What we hope is that you'll become a Wizard too, someone with the skills to take charge of your own learning and make things happen.

Introduction

WIZARDS HAVE THE KNOW-HOW

They've learned the secrets to learning. This knowledge amounts to a magic formula that can allow you to become a Wizard.

Learning is something you do naturally each and every day, whether in school or not. As Information becomes available you automatically take it in.

You absorb information all the time, without even intending you learn new things. You're a learning machine! So take advantage of that, make the machine work for you!

Let's define terms so we're all on the same page:

- **Learning** means you acquire facts, ideas, knowledge, information or master skills, etc. and make them yours.
- **Knowledge** means familiarity and understanding of a subject that you gain through experience or study.
- **Studying** refers to the methods you use to learn. These include: reading, taking notes, memorizing, practicing skills, etc.
- **A Skill** is competence and expertise, an ability you develop through study or learning and maintain with practice.

What to Expect

Scientists, the real "Wizards", study human learning to find out how people learn best. **A Wizard's Guide** is based on their research, on what actually works for people. By following the Guide the Wizard's secrets will become yours.

A Wizard's Guide to Study Skills will help you:

- Sharpen your focus and learn more efficient ways to study
- Develop the skills needed to enable you to better organize your homework & save time
- Increase your reading speed without lowering comprehension
- Gain more effective test-taking strategies to raise your test scores and grades

As you work with the **Wizard's Guide** you'll arrive at a place where studying becomes easier, that's what athletes call being in the zone. You'll be able to organize your time so that learning new material becomes much simpler and quicker. Just changing the ways you prepare for tests will, in itself, improve your grades.

Many students have used A Wizard's Guide to help them succeed. You can too, so let's begin!

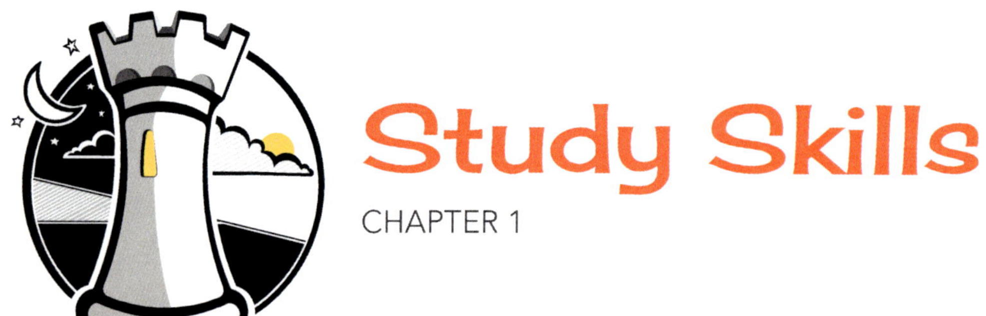

Study Skills

CHAPTER 1

SECRETS

Wizards have the Know-How because they really do know how! They've gained the secret knowledge of how to learn, the magic formula that can allow you to become a Wizard, an expert in whatever you want.

Kids like learning. It may sound funny especially when things come up in school but it's true. As we mentioned before human beings are learning machines, we're built for it. It's natural to enjoy learning new things. But sometimes we get stuck, we miss something or an explanation isn't clear. That's not unusual but it can be frustrating and can get you off track.

The whole idea of the **Wizard's Guide** is to share the knowledge that makes learning work. You'll stay on top of things and when something comes up it won't throw you. When you really understand how to study, homework will take less time so you'll be able to do more of what you enjoy. You'll get better test scores and your grades will improve. You'll make it happen! As you begin to feel better about your classes, you'll be less stressed out and, who knows, you may find that you enjoy learning too.

That's the Wizard's Way!

WHY LEARN HOW TO STUDY?

Skills are learned and studying is a skill.

Studying, like anything else can be learned, just like playing a sport or a musical instrument.

The difference is that study skills aren't usually taught; that's one of the secrets. Without a coach you're on your own.

> Imagine, while watching a baseball game for the first time someone throws you a ball and says, "Go play!" You may pick up some baseball skills, but trial and error learning has a major drawback: it's hit and miss. You'll tend to make mistakes and waste a lot of time trying things out before you get the knack.

The Wizard's Guide is designed so you can avoid some of the pitfalls common to the trial and error approach! The Guide is more like **having a personal coach.** It will show you better ways to study and save you lots of time.

You'll become a Study Skills Wizard!

HOMEWORK AND WHY WE NEED IT

Time is the challenge. There just isn't enough class time for teachers to present all the information you have to learn. That's why you're assigned chapters and online research so that you're able to cover everything you need to know.

Wizard's Tip

How you approach reading the chapters is important. The headings and textbook study questions serve as a useful guide. They highlight key concepts that you'll need to remember.

Skills improve with practice. As you're probably aware from sports and music, you need considerable practice to really excel. In the same way, homework builds skills by:

- Reinforcing your understanding of new material
- Providing extra time so you master more challenging topics
- Giving you the opportunity for practice

The organizational tools presented here will make homework flow more smoothly. The tools and concepts in the Guide will continue to be useful throughout your educational career, in high school and beyond.

STAYING FOCUSED

WIZARD'S TIP

How you study is important. You set aside Study Time **just for studying** and nothing else.

Staying focused is a major key to success!

Staying focused means avoiding distractions:

- NO phoning, texting, listening to music, TV or games!
- Shut it all off!
- A Wizard needs to focus!
- A Wizard allows NO interruptions!
- Wizards need their tools at hand!

Wizard's Tip

Be sure you have everything you need with you when you begin studying!

1. Your assignments
2. Textbooks
3. A tablet or computer
4. Any other necessary materials and supplies, some water etc.

Everything you'll need, pencils sharp, batteries charged

WIZARDS MAKE IT HAPPEN!

Things To Remember

1. Skills are learned and studying is a skill. _______________ and _______________ has its pitfalls.

2. A Wizard's Guide is like having a personal coach so you can save _______________ and become a _______________ _______________ _______________.

3. You set aside Study Time only for _______________.

4. Don't allow distractions, so you stay _______________.

5. Shut it all _______________.

6. It's important to have _______________ you _______________ before starting Study Time.

Answer

1. Trial error
2. time Study Skills Wizard
3. studying
4. focused
5. off
6. everything need

WHERE TO STUDY

Wizards in legend are often depicted in a tower or library surrounded by books and ancient scrolls. That was a special place where they could study and practice their magic. Wizards need a place to work. They may not have a tower but they always have what they need. That was the way of it and still is. Create your own space and make sure you have everything you need to work your magic.

- Wherever you study, **it's best to choose a quiet place.** That's essential when you're starting a brand new subject or skill.
- **It's better to study at a table or a desk, so you maintain focus and stay alert.** Sitting on a couch or easy chair lowers your concentration and breaks the spell. You'll be tempted to doze off or zone out.
- Even if it's only for your Study Time, you need to set up a convenient place to work whenever at home. **It's important so create a space that's yours, a dependable place where you're comfortable studying.**

Wizard's Tip

Having a well-organized, reliable place to work helps you settle in quicker and accomplish more. You'll associate that place with getting things done.

That's how the brain works.

Things To Remember

1. It's ideal to study in a ______________ ______________.

2. You can concentrate better at a ______________ or a ______________.

3. If you always study in the ______________ ______________ you'll get in the ______________ and accomplish ______________.

Answer

1. quiet place
2. table desk
3. same place zone more

Memory Strategies

CHAPTER 2

HOW TO STUDY

Memorizing dates, tables, or formulas isn't anyone's favorite task, but we all know a certain amount of memorization is necessary. Even though we've come to rely on technology, for example computers, search engines, tablets, phones, and even watches, we still need to be able to memorize on our own.

Scientists, real Wizards, have studied learning and memory for some time. We're beginning to understand how memories are formed and stored. Based on these insights educators have developed a number of approaches that work. Here are a few you can try.

Here's a shortcut to use when learning to spell vocabulary words:

1. Write the first word on the list in pen.
2. Trace over that word in pencil, saying each letter aloud as you write it.
3. Next copy the word twice, repeating each letter **aloud**.
4. Then cover all the words you've written and write the first word from memory, saying each letter **silently** to yourself as you write it.
5. If you spell the word correctly, repeat the same process with the remaining words.
6. If you misspell a word, just repeat steps 3 and 4 before going on to the next word.

After you finish the list, it's a great idea to test yourself again just to be sure you've got them all.

WHY THIS WORKS

Writing, saying and hearing the words simultaneously consolidates information in memory.

This approach activates multiple parts of the brain at once creating new connections. Scientists today can even demonstrate these processes in "real time."

This multisensory approach is a dependable way to memorize anything you need to learn; Science, Math, Sports, anything.

Consider how you can use this technique for other things.

A clever way to improve your test scores is to vary the order whenever you study vocabulary and definitions.

WIZARD'S TIP

Rather than studying from a list, Wizards write each word on a **separate index card.**

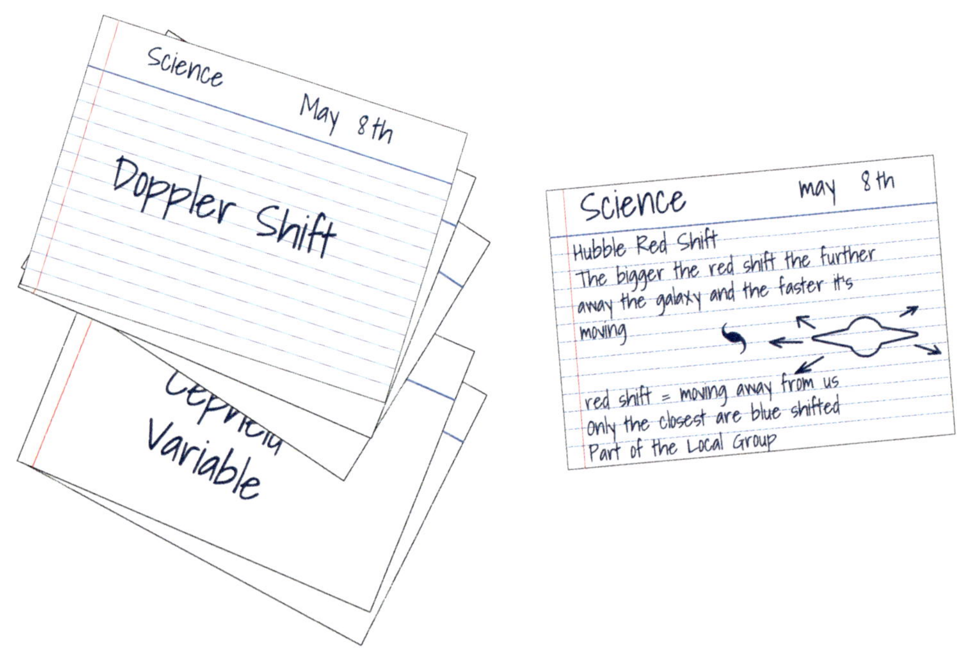

Since the words can come at you in any sequence on a test, you gain an advantage by also studying and reviewing them in a random order. Wizards know better ways to study so they score higher on tests. Not studying from a list keeps you a step ahead.

After you finish studying, it's a great idea to test yourself again just to be sure you've got them all down.

This works! It's exercise for your brain.

Of course using this same technique makes learning definitions a snap too! The word you're studying is on the front side of the index card and its definition is on the reverse.

FOCUSED READING & ACTIVE LEARNING

Most students start each new assignment by **reading the entire chapter first and then answering the Study Questions.** Studies show it's much more effective to read the questions first and then search for the answers in the chapter. That saves time and effort because you know what you're looking for. Be sure you understand the questions. **Reading the questions first ensures that you learn faster and remember better.**

Actively searching to find the answer is the first step. Once you find it, the next step is to **ask yourself the same question and see if you remember the answer!**

Here's the whole sequence:

- Start by reading over the first Study Question.
- Then, search through the text to find the answer, write it down, and make sure it's correct.
- Next quiz yourself. Cover the answer and see if you can remember it correctly. No peeking!

Actively trying to recall the answer helps strengthen your memory.

Follow the same steps with the remaining questions. After you've answered all the Study Questions, read over the chapter to be certain you haven't missed anything important. It is that simple and now you know how!

MEMORY STRATEGIES

Scientists have shown that memory actually improves with practice.

Studies demonstrate that actively **remembering what you've just learned** helps store that information in long term memory. Then it's easier to remember on a test. Things you learn but don't think about tend to fade with time and become harder and harder to recall. That's why Math fades so fast if you don't practice the skills.

Wise Wizards use the methods we've described to speed up learning and boost memory: **So remember to take a moment to recall new facts and skills right after learning them!**

TAKING NOTES

Teachers in your school may recommend/require that students follow a particular note taking system.

One widely used system is **Cornell Notes.** If your teachers don't require that you follow a particular approach, the Cornell method is one many Wizards find useful. It's a good option.

Cornell Notes was developed in the 1950s at Cornell University and is widely used from middle school through college in the US. A description of the basic system can be found here: https://en.wikipedia.org/wiki/Cornell_Notes

Geology
chp 6

Keywords:	Notes:
	Types of Rocks
Igneous	1. Igneous formed through cooling & solidification of magma/lava.
Sedimentary	2. Sedimentary formed from sediment in rivers lakes oceans - may have fossils
Metamorphic	3. Metamorphic Transformed by heat/pressure

Summary
three main rock types

Our Wizard's Notes form in Appendix A is compatible with Cornell Notes.

TIPS FOR TAKING NOTES

Most students use abbreviations when taking lecture notes because they think it's faster.

For example:

Absolute Zero = theor. temp. @ which all molec. motion stops

The complete sentence would be:

Absolute Zero = The theoretical temperature at which all molecular motion stops.

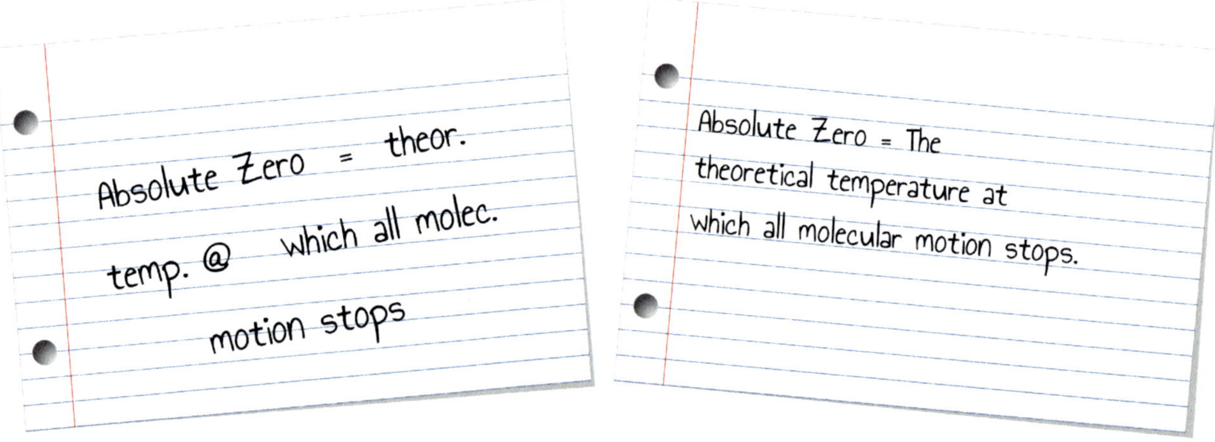

The complete definition is longer, but it's easier to memorize because you don't have to decode it.

Abbreviations may make note taking seem faster, but when you read them later on there's a good chance it'll be harder to remember what they mean. **There's no reason to make studying more difficult.**

If possible your notes should capture the complete meaning of the material being presented. If you use abbreviations, take time to copy your notes out as complete sentences while you still remember them. **This will help a lot when reviewing for a test.**

The Wizard's Notes and Wizard's Research Notes forms found in **Appendix A** will help.

Wizard's techniques work because they're based on a deep understanding of the brain and how we process data.

When you start using them, be prepared to be amazed!

Wizard's Tip

If you miss a class, remember to **ask a friend** for copies of the day's notes. Your teacher may have covered new material not in your textbook. **It may be on the exam!**

Things To Remember

1. Memory improves with ________________.

2. Actively trying to remember what you just studied improves your ________________.

3. When learning ________________ and ________________, Wizards recommend ________________ them in a ________________ order.

4. With textbook assignments, it's best to ________________ all the Study Questions ________________.

5. When taking notes, remember it's more effective to study for tests using ________________ ________________ than abbreviations.

1. practice
2. memory
3. vocabulary definitions studying random
4. answer first
5. complete sentences

Reading Speed

CHAPTER 3

WHAT IS READING SPEED?

What do we mean by Reading Speed? Wizards know that how fast you're able to read directly impacts how long it takes to complete assignments. Slow reading speed will cost you a lot of time. Making even a small improvement can save you hours!

What about "Speed Reading"? Speed reading, just usually another word for "skimming", isn't a good idea. You can glance over reading material using speed reading, but it won't really improve your studying at all. In fact, **trying to learn new material using speed reading actually lowers comprehension.**

Average reading speed is measured in words per minute (wpm). Your speed determines how long it will take you to read something. Of course, reading speed isn't constant and varies with the difficulty level of the material. Some subjects like science, social studies and literature require a higher level of reading concentration. In that case, you may need to read more slowly.

Adults generally read at about 300 words per minute (wpm). Middle school and high school students generally average about 150 wpm with 65% comprehension. It can get better!

- Each time your eyes come to rest as you read across a line of text is called an **eye fixation.**
- The **number of eye fixations per line** is a major component of reading speed.

- Reading **word for word** can really slow you down.
- As a result, doing homework takes much longer!

If you have a habit of stopping to read every single word across a line you'll need **extra time** to complete assignments, time you could better use for something else!

IMPROVING YOUR AVERAGE READING SPEED

Wizards have a simple technique that'll help you **increase** your reading speed. First, let's see what it's like if you stop to read one word at a time. Read the following sentence aloud:

One very simple way to increase your reading speed Is to use fewer eye fixations.

Notice how this really slows things down?

The simplest way to increase your average reading speed is to read a group of words at once. Instead of reading word for word, **reading two (or more) words with each eye fixation can double your reading speed** at the very least.

Increasing your reading speed will save you an amazing amount of time!

Now, let's practice reading by grouping 2 words at a time. This way you'll read faster as you're not stopping to read each individual word.

One very simple way to increase your reading speed is to look at a group of two words at a time, so you can experience how much faster you are able to read text.

By progressing to group 3 words at a time you have even fewer eye fixations. Your eyes will move across the line even more quickly. Give it a try:

In order to increase your reading speed, even more, you can now see and read a group of three words at a time. Continuing to do this can increase your reading speed up to 200%!

That's the way you'll increase your reading speed! Now Nail it!

With practice, grouping two or more words at a time will become second nature and your reading speed will improve. You'll be amazed how reading becomes almost effortless and your reading enjoyment grows.

You can do it!

Think about this, if you train yourself to group words and begin to read two at a time you've effectively **doubled your reading speed!!**

WIZARD'S TIP

Some people have a habit of saying words in their head while reading (subvocalizing). It's one of the main reasons people read slowly. Your mind can process language much faster than this. **Focus on seeing 2-3 words at a time.**

Research shows there's no disadvantage to increasing your reading speed. As long as you're not skimming, your reading comprehension won't change.

This technique is one of the simplest ways to read faster!!

Note: Appendix B contains a selection from "Alice's Adventures in Wonderland" by Lewis Carroll. It's presented several ways to give you extra practice in grouping words as you read. Enjoy making progress!

Things To Remember

1. Skimming is another word for ______________ ______________.

2. Reading speed is determined primarily by the number of ______________ ______________ per ______________.

3. By seeing ______________ or more words per eye fixation you'll be able to at least ______________ your reading speed without ______________ your ______________.

Answer

1. speed reading
2. eye fixations line
3. two double lowering comprehension

Homework

CHAPTER 4

YOUR APPROACH MATTERS

Wizards know that homework is a fact of life. There's more work than ever and classroom time is limited. Homework is your teacher's only way to be sure you have an opportunity to cover all the material. It's why they assign outside reading and online research.

Most students see homework just as something to "get through". They choose to view it as meaningless and boring.

There is a different way.

Homework may seem boring, but only if you decide it is. Your viewpoint is what counts. You might want to reconsider what homework is really about. It's up to you.

THE RATIONALE

So, what is the positive side of homework?

- **First**, it's the only way to cover everything. It's also a way for you to discover and explore on your own. What you discover for yourself has a way of sticking with you. Discovery is what humans are all about.

- **Second**, it's about building skills and getting practice. From math to art to sports, practice is what you need to do to understand and get good at something. The only way to really learn how to do something is to do it.

Wizards understand that **skills improve with practice**. That's the name of the game. Becoming good at anything, like sports and music or dance, requires practice and real concentration. It takes work but it's worth the effort.

That's what homework is about!

So we can agree that:

- Homework serves to reinforce your understanding of material you've just learned in class.
- It provides the time you'll need to master more challenging topics.
- It's an opportunity to practice and improve your skills.
- It gives you a chance to dig into something deeper, to explore and expand your horizons.

Guess what? Wizards have discovered ways to make homework flow more smoothly!

HOMEWORK HOW-TO

Homework can work "for" you if you let it. For example, let your teacher know right away if you don't fully understanding an assignment.

A Wizard knows when to get help.

Sometimes homework assignments may seem too easy or boring. If that happens, don't laugh, consider requesting more interesting/challenging work for extra credit.

Studies show that **students are more alert and have higher concentration at the start of a homework session**. As a clever Wizard, you can use that fresher energy to your advantage. **Tackle the most difficult assignments first**. More often than not, the subject you'll decide to start with will be **Math**.

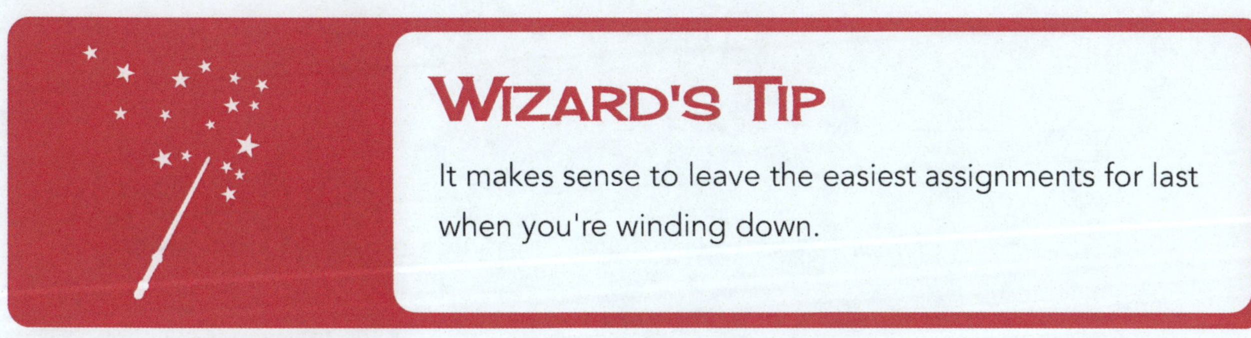

Studying smart makes you a Wizard.

Things To Remember

1. Homework is necessary because there isn't enough ____________ for teachers to present all the ____________ during class.

2. Outside ____________ and online ____________ are assigned to ____________ in classroom learning.

3. Skills improve with ____________.

4. Students are most alert and able to ____________ ____________ at the ____________ of a homework session.

5. Take advantage of your higher energy level, so begin homework sessions by working on the most ____________ ____________ first.

6. It makes sense to leave the ____________ subject for last because that one requires ____________ effort.

Answer

1.	time	information	
2.	reading	research	supplement
3.	practice		
4.	concentrate	best	start
5.	difficult	assignment	
6.	easiest	less	

MATH IS SPECIAL

Math requires ongoing practice in order to develop and maintain excellent problem solving skills. Without the benefit of homework you probably wouldn't ever practice doing Math. Math just gets rusty very quickly!

Wizard's Tip

Research shows that how you go about doing your Math homework is as important as getting it done. Even if you're unsure about how to proceed, don't be afraid to try.

You've heard the saying, "Practice makes perfect." Well with Math, **"Only perfect practice makes perfect!."**

Before you begin to tackle a brand new assignment, work the first few problems to make sure you understand the new concepts.

Think about it: if you practice doing something the wrong way what do you learn? You need to understand how to solve Math correctly!

When doing Math homework **it's important to "get it"** before you start. If you're not sure you understand, try to solve the first couple of problems in class. Then ask your teacher to look over your work to be sure you get it. **It's your job to ask.**

Wizard's Way

Research shows that **anyone can learn Math well.** You don't need to be a "Math genius".

Studies show that **students who believe they can do Math actually demonstrate higher Math achievement.**

You really need to believe in yourself;
You can do Math!

Don't be shy! If you're not sure how to proceed, there may be others that don't get it as well. **A Wizard knows when to ask for help.** Do everyone a favor, raise your hand.

Just checking your work over for errors then making corrections can really improve your understanding, and how well you'll do.

Catching your mistakes and correcting them is one of the main keys to conquering Math.

How you approach Math homework is just as important as getting it done. Here are the Wizard's four essential keys to Math success:

1. **First, you need to firmly believe that you can do Math.** It doesn't matter whether or not you're a Math genius. **Just having confidence in your ability can raise your achievement level.**

2. If there's something you don't understand, **ask your teacher to explain things so you get it.**

3. Remember that with Math, "**Only Perfect Practice makes Perfect!**"

4. To improve your understanding try to **always check your own work** and **make any necessary corrections.**

WIZARD'S WAY

Everyone makes Math errors. It's essential to understand how to work the problems in order to solve them correctly!

There's no "wiggle room" in Math!

Things To Remember

1. Math requires ongoing ________________.

2. With Math only ________________ practice makes ________________.

3. If you don't understand something ________________ for ________________.

4. If you ________________ you can do Math you ________________!

5. Checking over your Math to find ________________ and ________________ them improves your ________________.

Answer 

1. practice
2. perfect perfect
3. ask help
4. believe can
5. errors correcting understanding

LEARNING AND SLEEP

Research on how we approach studying reveals some very interesting findings about brain function. For example, we now know why sleep is critical. Your bedtime routine can directly affect your test performance the next day.

You need downtime of at least 30 minutes off the screen after you finish studying before bed! New research shows that any screen time during the last 1/2 hour before bed interferes with both sleep and learning. (That also includes your phone!) In fact, research subjects who stay up that extra half hour and don't go straight to sleep score significantly lower on tests the next day.

So when you're done studying the night before a test, turn off the computer and go to bed.

WIZARD'S TIP

A solid night's sleep can make better than a full grade's difference on your test score.

Study hard, get to bed early, then... Nail It!

The Matrix

CHAPTER 5

MANAGE YOUR TIME

Time Management is nothing less than the Wizard's Secret, it's what enables the magic to happen.

You've probably heard the term before. Business people use it all the time, it's the process of organizing what you do. You already manage your time without thinking about it.

You get up in the morning to an alarm clock you've set the night before. You brush your teeth, get dressed and have breakfast all in time to catch the bus. Your classes run on a schedule: homeroom, Math, then lunch, then more classes in the afternoon. Catch the bus again. Then chores, a trip to the store, homework, dinner, probably more homework and bed. That's the routine. It's natural, you don't even think about it.

But what if you do?...

Good time management ensures you'll work smarter, not harder.

Actively managing your time lets you get all the things you need and want to do done. The same thing that gets you off to school on time is what gets a spaceship to Mars. You know exactly what you're going to be doing.

Major goals become attainable because of what you do every day, because of how you've planned. You'll even be able to find more time to spend with the people that matter to you. Then when things come up you have the tools to manage them.

PLAN AND TAKE IT ONE STEP AT A TIME!

That's what will make you a Wizard

Let's get started.

Wizards know there's only so much time in a day. It's important to be efficient if you want to accomplish all the things you'd like to do. You need a plan to manage your time!

Following a schedule makes studying simpler because things are organized. An easy-to-follow plan ensures great results so homework doesn't drag on.
Let's find out how that works!

Things To Remember

1. Good ________________ ________________ helps you work ________________.

2. Actively ________________ your time lets you get things ________________.

3. Wizards know that following a ________________ makes ________________ simpler.

Answer 

1. time management smarter
2. managing done
3. schedule studying

WEEKLY ASSIGNMENT MATRIX

As a student, you attend classes on a schedule. Your teachers present material according to lesson plans and that works just fine. Wouldn't it be great to use that same structured approach with your homework? You can!

Most likely you already write down your assignments. Using the **Weekly Assignment Matrix** gives you an advantage. It makes keeping track of homework and completing assignments on time much simpler.

The Weekly Assignment Matrix gives you an instant overview of what you need to accomplish day by day.

Beginning on Monday, the 1st day of each week, you'll list all your daily homework and study assignments by subject. There are spaces for up to 6 subjects each day.

Having your assignments in a Matrix keeps you on target! Take time to write it out neatly and accurately; record everything you need. **Remember you're creating your own tools, so make sure they work!**

WIZARD'S TIP

Teachers usually post homework on the board. Use your phone to snap a picture of the day's assignments.

Here's an example of the **Weekly Assignment Matrix.**

WIZARDS GUIDES®- WEEKLY ASSIGNMENT MATRIX

Name: Kyle P   Week of: 3/4/19

MON   TUE   WED

Subjects

Math page 68 even prob 6 - 16

English questions 4-6 pg 70

Science Astro Chap 5 Questions 3&6

Social Studies Read chap 6 Answer Q1 - 5

STUDY ALERTS!

Planets rpt - Mars draft due on the 8th

STUDY GRP AT JOHN'S SATURDAY 12 to 3

Math quiz on the 8th

Monday's Date

List daily assignments here. Include all the information you'll need

For reminders about what's happening in school this week, tests, due dates, things you want to remember

Be neat! You're creating your own tools, make sure they work for you!

...ds available at KidsLikeLearning.com/resources
...mons Licensing Attribution-NonCommercial-NoDerivs.
...se & share with other students!

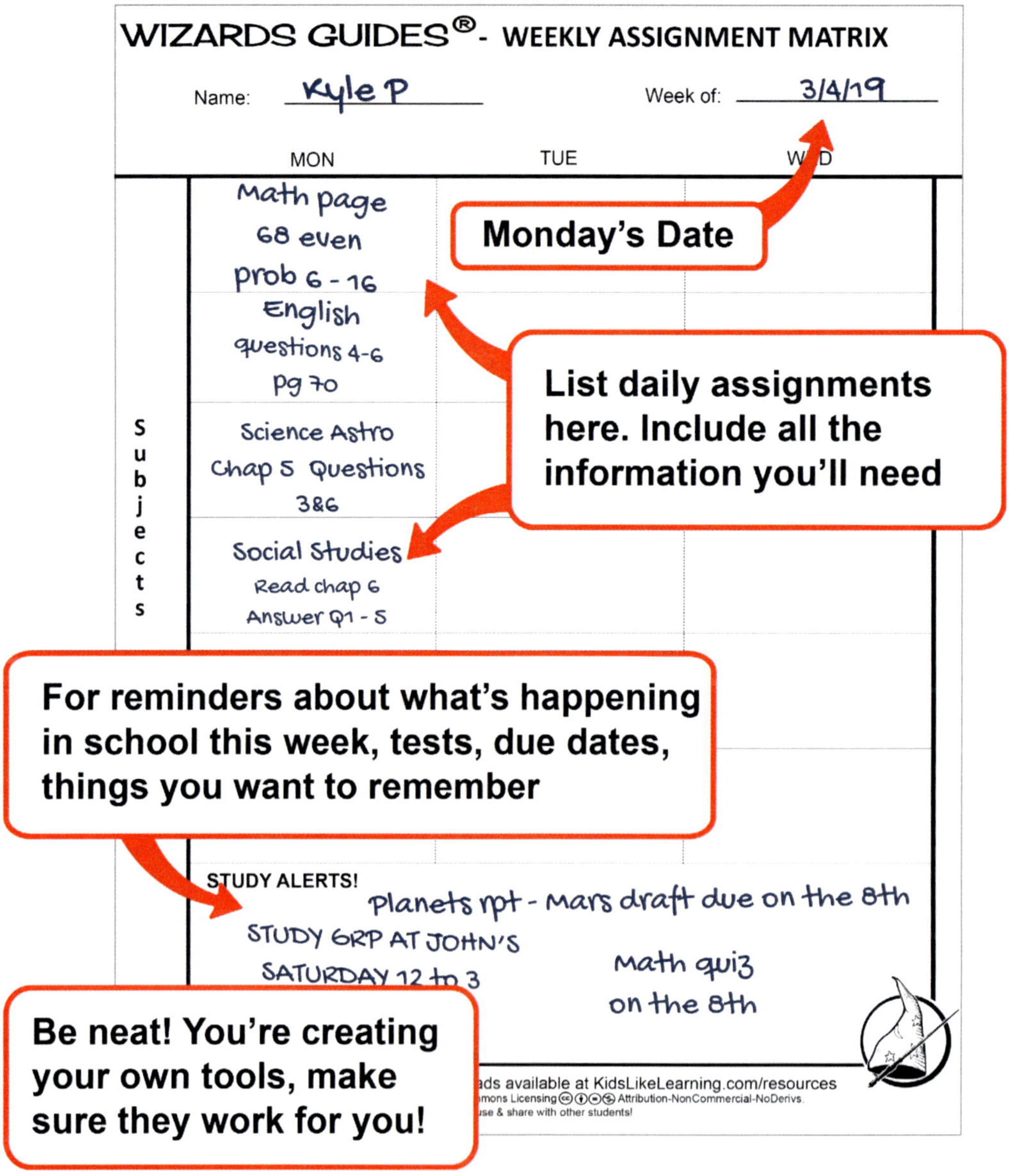

Nowadays you'll find your homework assignments are often posted to a website, along with other materials. Make sure you know how to access them. **Speak up if you're having problems logging in**.

A Wizard uses the tools at hand.

STUDY ALERTS!

Notice the Study Alerts! section at the bottom of the form.

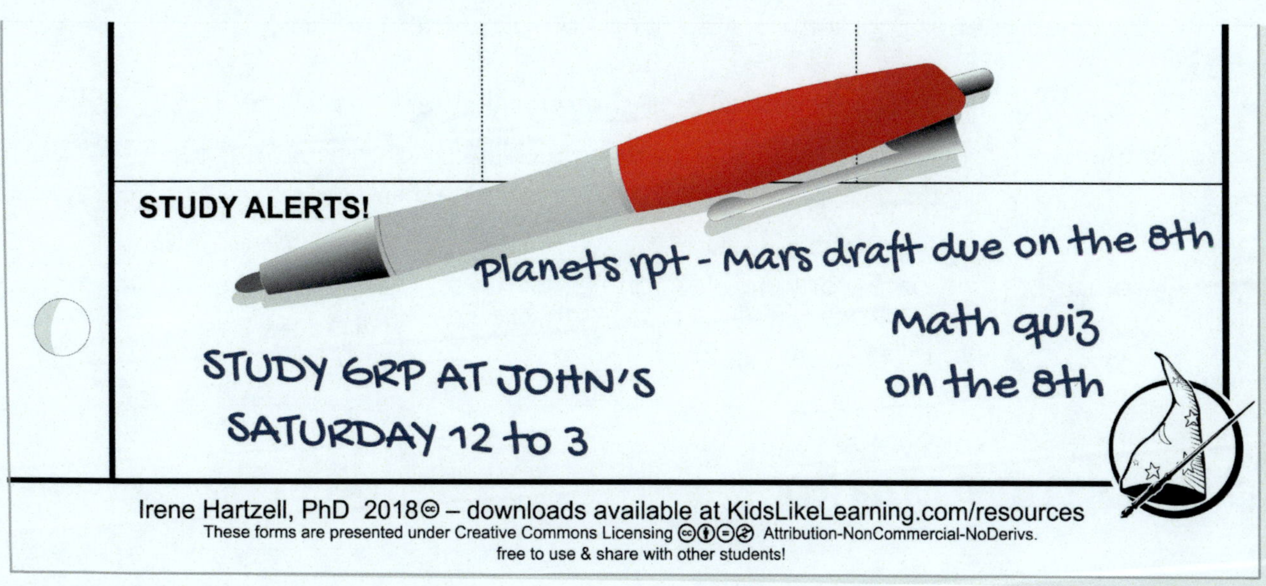

That's where you'll jot down all the important things you need to remember during that week, like reminders about upcoming assignments, tests and quizzes. Perhaps you plan to work with a friend or you're in a study group? Put that information here too. Now you have everything you need in one place.

Using "Study Alerts!" will help keep you on track.

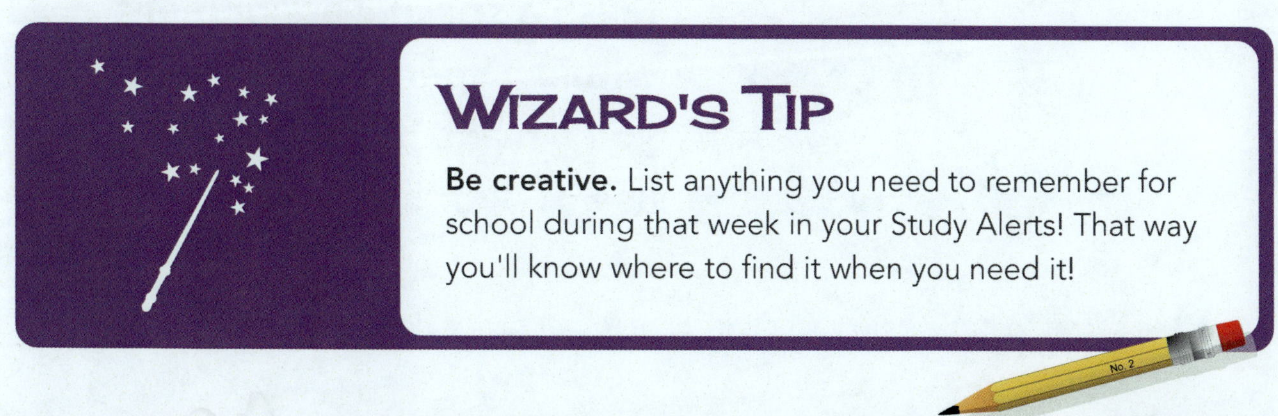

WIZARD'S TIP

Be creative. List anything you need to remember for school during that week in your Study Alerts! That way you'll know where to find it when you need it!

Study Alerts! will help you:

- Remember tests you need to prepare for
- Know when your assignments are due and complete them on time
- Schedule additional time for longer assignments like papers and reports (Remember, your teacher won't be giving you daily assignments on these, it's easy to get behind)
- Keep track of due dates for longer assignments

DAILY STUDY MATRIX

Now we come to the daily component of the**Wizard's System.** This is what's going to keep you on track with your homework.

It's the key!

Assignments that should take only 30 minutes can extend to hours if you're not careful. The Daily Study Matrix will help you stay focused so you get the job done.

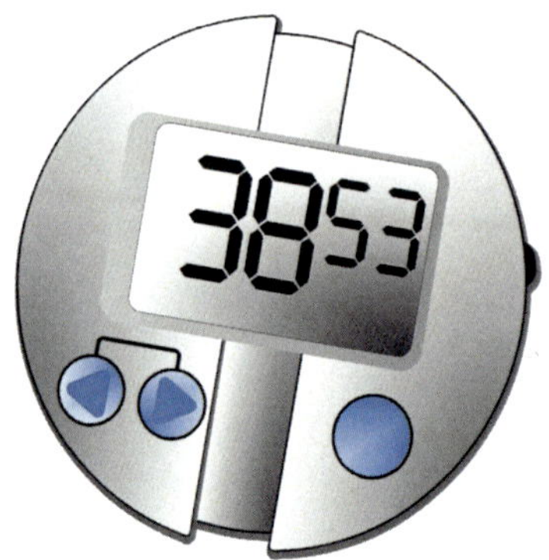

If you make it your goal to finish a specific assignment within a specific timeframe, you'll make much better use of your study time.

This is the secret to optimizing your study time to get things done it's how the brain works.

Not only will you get a handle on your homework and finish it but you'll remember the material better.

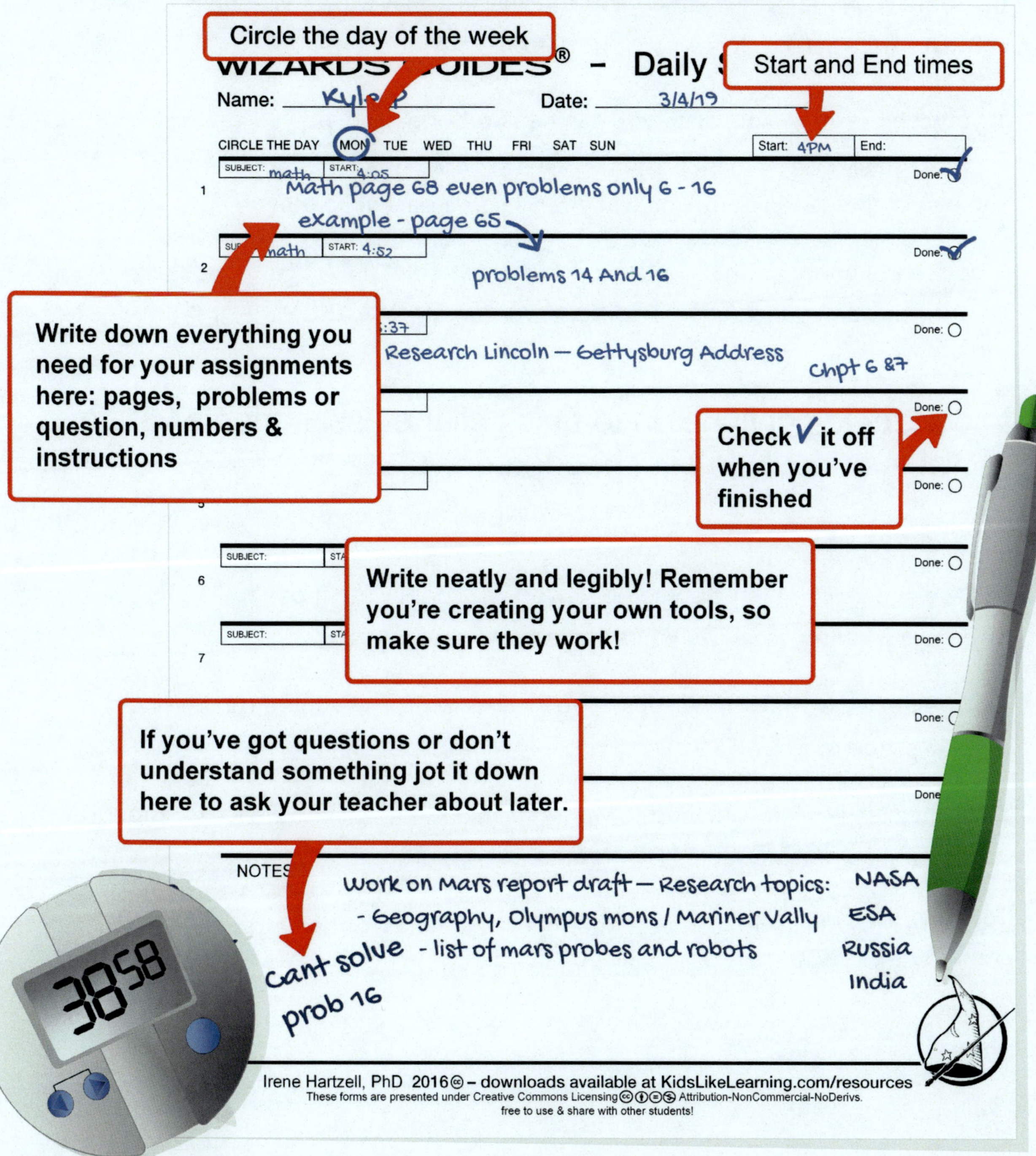

Note: You'll need to set a timer to work with the Daily Study Matrix. Any timer will do, even an old fashioned kitchen timer.

Working with the **Daily Study Matrix** you'll copy down each assignment one at a time. You have the most energy when you start your homework. That's a fact, so it makes sense to get the more challenging subjects out of the way first. Save the easier ones for last. Exercise breaks between study sessions will help keep your energy up.

1. If you come across a question you can't answer or a problem you can't solve try to get some help. If you still can't solve it, go on and try to finish the rest of the assignment. You can always come back to it later.

2. If you're still hung up on something, make a note of it (In the Notes section) and check with your teacher as soon as you can.

It's important to continue on to finish all the assignments you're able to do. Don't get bogged down!

3. In case you've completed some homework in school write it down and mark it off the list. Give yourself credit.

4. On the next row write in the subject you'll start with. This should be the one that takes the most brain power. (Probably Math)

5. Copy in exactly what you need to work on. "Do Math" just isn't specific enough. You'll want something more like: "Math - pg. 43, probs 1 - 15," to stay on target!

6. Estimate how much you can accomplish in 40 minutes. Set your goal! Add in your start time and set your timer! Then get to work!

7. See where you are in 40 minutes when the timer goes off.

    - If you're finished, great
    - If you finish early take your break or move on to the next assignment
    - Whatever the subject, some assignments take more than 40 minutes. If anything's left, move it down to the section below and complete it in the next period.

8. Either way, check it off ✓. You've worked for 40 minutes!

9. Next set your timer and enjoy your break.

10. It's important to complete all the assignments that you can. Don't get bogged down!

    - If you come across a question and you're stumped get help if you can.
    - If you still can't solve it, jot it down in 'Notes' to check with your teacher the next day.
    - Then go on to finish the rest of your assignment. You can always come back later to something you might have skipped.

11. Follow these same steps for the rest of your homework.

The Wizard's System also works just fine with reading and research assignments. Reading for 40 minutes then exercising keeps you fresh.

Check out **Chapter 2 Memory Strategies** above for ways to use focused reading and active learning for improving recall.

Managing your time well is a Wizard's skill that gives you the edge throughout high school and beyond!

WIZARDS GUIDES® - Daily Study Matrix

Name: Kyle P   Date: 3/4/18

CIRCLE THE DAY (MON) TUE WED THU FRI SAT SUN   Start: 4PM   End:

1 SUBJECT: math   START: 4:05   Done: ✓
Math page 68 even problems only 6 - 16
example - page 65

2 SUBJECT: math   START: 4:52   Done: ✓
problems 14 And 16

3 SUBJECT: Am Hist   START: 5:37   Done: ○
Research Lincoln — Gettysburg Address
Chpt 6 &7

4 SUBJECT: START:

5 SUBJECT: START:

6 SUBJECT: START: Done: ○

7 SUBJECT: Done: ○

8   Done: ○

9 SUBJECT: Done: ○

NOTES

Work on Mars report draft — Research topics: NASA
- Geography, Olympus mons / Mariner vally ESA
- list of mars probes and robots Russia
India

Cant solve prob 16

Irene Hartzell, PhD 2018 – downloads available at KidsLikeLearning.com/resources

"A Wizard is Never Late."— Gandalf the Grey

Estimating what you can accomplish within a given time is a true Wizard's skill. Try not to overload your 40 minutes. At first, you may find you overestimate how much you think you can complete during a study period, but that's ok. After you gain experience you'll be able to accurately allocate the time needed for each assignment. That's a useful knack.

When the timer goes off after studying 40 minutes, switch gears and take a 5-minute break to get some aerobic exercise. Aerobic means you'll be up and moving!

You just need to get your heart pumping, this gets oxygen flowing to the brain. An active study break will ensure you feel refreshed and better able to concentrate on your next assignment.

You can choose any aerobic activity or a combination, like dancing, jumping jacks, skipping rope, etc. Be creative and have fun!

WIZARD'S TIP

Research shows if you get regular exercise you'll have better concentration and get better grades. **So go out and do something you enjoy!** It doesn't matter what: dance, play a sport, run or walk on a daily basis. Just do it. **Our bodies are meant to move!**

Note: Check with your parents before undertaking exercise to make sure you are exercising safely and in accordance with applicable medical advice.

There are other resources where you can get help with your homework if you get stuck. You can find a list of them at **https://KidsLikeLearning.com/Guides**.

The Daily Study Matrix is there for you. Use it to keep on track. It's your tool and it's flexible. For example, if you come to the end of a study session and have a few problems left or a paragraph to read feel free to continue. You can set the timer for a couple of minutes but when you're in the zone sometimes you just want to finish!

Don't forget to also schedule time for all the reading and research assignments in the Daily Study Matrix. Taking aerobic breaks really helps your focus with longer reading assignments too.

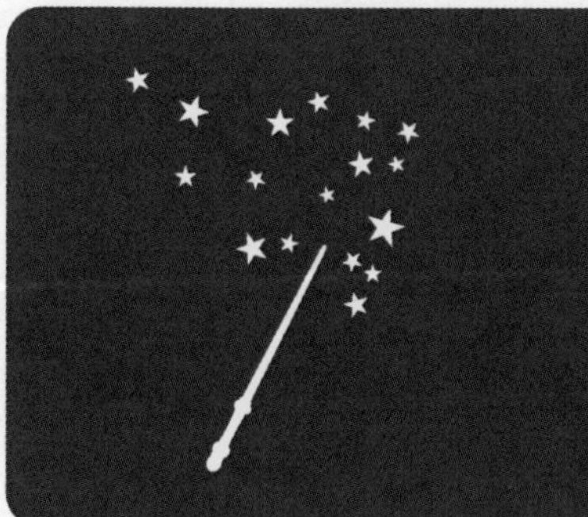

WIZARD'S TIP

Wizards know when to be flexible!
Experiment. Think about what works best for you and try things out! If you figure out something good, share it.

If you have homework or need to study over the weekend, continue using the Daily Study Matrix as usual.

There's one important exception to working the hardest assignments first: On the night before a test, always reserve the last study session(s) for **test prep and review**, even if it's a Math test!

WIZARD'S TIP

Research shows that **what we study right before sleep sticks best.**

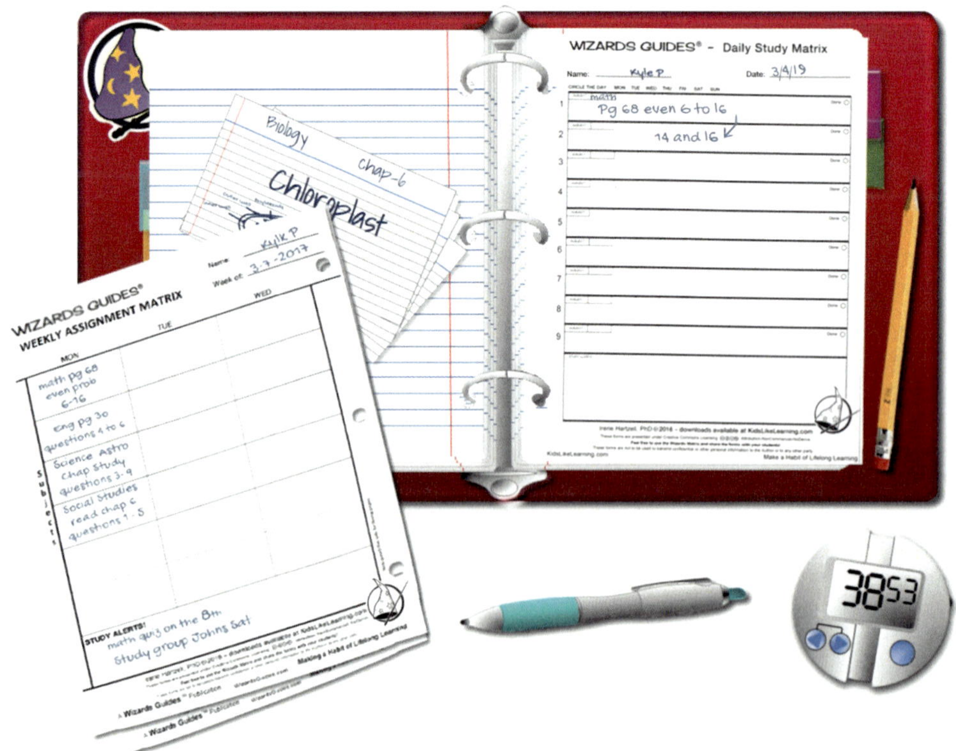

Setting and meeting specific study goals will keep you focused. You'll gain an immediate sense of accomplishment as you do your homework. **Don't forget to check off each session as you complete it!** When your homework flows you'll stay energized and **in the zone.**

Feel free to fine tune the Wizard's methods to suit the way you work. Just remember to take those regular 5-minute breaks and move your body to stay revved up. You're in charge of your own schedule, so decide what works best for you. It really helps to have a system!

What Wizards do works. Give it a try!

When you've finished your homework take a breath. Look over what you've done. Each study session checked off shows what you've accomplished.

Be sure all your papers are ready to hand in. You nailed it!

Things To Remember

1. The ________________ ________________ Matrix gives you an instant overview of what you need to accomplish day by day.

2. The ________________ ________________ section is where you'll jot down anything important you need to ________________ for school that week.

3. The ________________ ________________ Matrix keeps you on track while doing your homework assignments.

4. The Daily Study Matrix is divided into ________________ minute study sessions followed by 5 minutes of ________________ ________________.

Answer

1. Weekly Assignment
2. Study Alerts! remember
3. Daily Study
4. 40 aerobic exercise

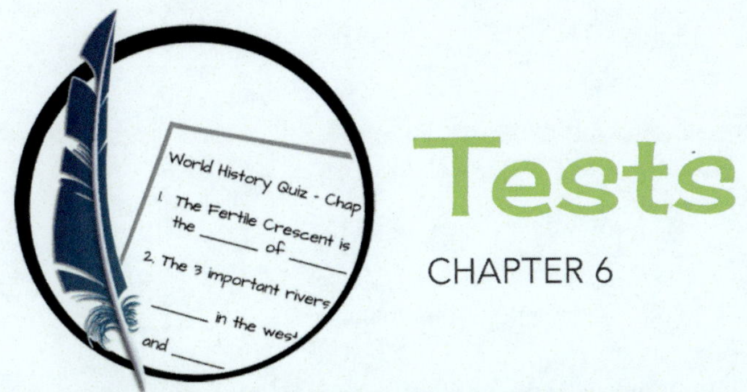

Tests

CHAPTER 6

WHY TESTS

Testing is just part of the academic assessment process, the way schools measure both teaching and learning. Test results give you feedback on how you're doing. Use them to see where you need to focus your efforts to get the results you want. Just like homework, tests are a fact of life. Even though some students dread testing, Wizards know how to handle stress.

Here's what you can do to approach tests with more confidence:

1. Continue using the Wizard's study tools and keep up in class so you don't get so swamped. That way you won't have to cram.
2. Learn simple research-based techniques that Wizards use to reduce stress.
3. Understand how tests work and use that knowledge to your advantage.

TEST PREPARATION

Wizard's Tip

How you study directly affects test performance. Wizards know, and research shows, that cramming just doesn't work well.

It's best to avoid cramming altogether. Whether or not you've been studying all along, staying up really late the night before only adds stress. That has a negative impact on how well you do on your test.

If you decide you have to cram, be aware that what you study may work just for the test, but it won't stick. You won't retain that information when you need it later.

So, when you prepare for tests remember: Avoid cramming!

You know what to do:

1. Set a regular schedule to study ahead of time and complete all the assignments.

2. Space your study sessions across several days.

3. Summarize your notes for review; it's really a good technique.

4. **Schedule review time the night before a test. Then go straight to sleep afterward.** Studies prove that students who do this perform better on exams the next day. The subjects who stay up longer "after studying" score significantly lower. We'll talk about this more in the section on Preparing for Tests.

5. Get a good night's sleep and have breakfast in the morning for an added advantage. Your brain needs rest and fuel to perform well!

HANDLING STRESS

A Wizard's ultimate goal is real know-how. If you haven't had any time to study, cramming may help you answer some questions and pass a test. The problem is that you won't remember what you've learned. Our brains don't work like that; what you cram in has a way of spilling out and that's information you'll probably need later. As Wizards, you're learning how to study, you'll be an expert at it.

Remember to stay calm, it's only a test! It helps to keep tests in perspective; there will be others... lots of them! Try to keep sight of the bigger picture. Also, if you're just starting out with the **Wizard's Guide**, be assured that, like with any new skill, you'll improve with practice!

GET IN THE ZONE

Sometimes remaining calm right before a test is easier said than done. Lots of students get tense and nervous. You're not alone. Think about it, other people have found ways to deal with this kind of stress. There's even a name for it: "performance anxiety." Wouldn't it be great to handle tension the way professional athletes do? Their secret is to practice hard ahead of time. Then, before a game, they find their focus and use breathing techniques to **get in the zone!**

If you've done a good job of studying, you won't be stressed and that's the best antidote for test anxiety.

Fitness and making the grade

One of the simplest, most effective ways to deal with stress is exercise. People are built to move and our bodies expect it. Inactivity affects the balance of chemicals in the brain. Lack of exercise will make you feel tired and rundown. Research shows that most people don't get nearly enough exercise. We drive places and sit in front of screens most of the day. On average we walk a lot less than people did 50 years ago, this is true for all ages.

Mens sana in corpore sano.
Latin: "a sound mind in a sound body"

The body and mind are connected, this is both ancient wisdom and modern science. It makes sense.

Activity is especially important for young people, physical and mental health both suffer if you don't move! The good news is you don't need a special or extreme regimen to get back in balance.

Research has shown that immediate benefits are gained from something as simple as walking. Take a brisk walk and clear your mind. Think about your breathing or count your steps, one, two, one, two, and you'll come back feeling refreshed and energized.

Note: Check with your parents before undertaking exercise to make sure you are exercising safely and in accordance with applicable medical advice.

So, take time to walk whenever you can, and If possible, walk or bike to school. Enjoy being outdoors, playing sports or dancing to your music. Get together with some friends and do some activities.

WIZARD'S TIP

Make being active a part of your daily life.
Wizards know it makes a huge difference.

NUTRITION AND CHOICES

What you eat affects how well you learn. Start the day with a good breakfast and drink enough water throughout the day to stay hydrated.

Breakfast is important, remember you've been asleep for at least eight hours and probably have at least four hours to go until lunch. Your body needs fuel! Even if you're running late grab a banana or a couple of slices of cheese, just make sure you eat.

The same goes for **Hydration**. After you've been asleep all night you need to top off the tanks. Water is particularly important for brain function. Many doctors and coaches recommend two full glasses of water when you wake up. Making sure you drink sufficient water during the day keeps you more alert.

You can't always choose what you eat, but Wizards know the choices they do have can make a difference. Foods with refined sugars will give you a quick boost but you crash just as quickly! Healthy snacks make more sense. When it comes to staying hydrated, water works much better than soda. It doesn't mean "never" eat candy or drink soda but be aware.

Note: Check with your parents and be aware of your diet and any restrictions

BREATHING

When you're nervous you tend to take quick, shallow breaths. Shallow breathing lowers the oxygen flow to your body, particularly to your brain. You'll feel tense and uncomfortable.

- According to Andrew Weil, M.D.,"Practicing regular, mindful breathing can be calming and energizing."
- **Breathing exercises work to help you de-stress.**
  As you proceed with doing the exercises you'll notice your breath flows more smoothly. Your mind will calm down, you'll be able to focus.
- Studies show that using breathing exercises before an exam can lower test anxiety and improve test scores.
- Mindful breathing can be even more beneficial if you make it part of your daily routine.

Here's how you'll do it:

Begin by taking a slow, steady breath in through your nose while counting silently from **1** to **4**. Then exhale slowly through your mouth, again counting silently to **4**.

Practicing steady, slow, even breathing is key.

You'll want to pay close attention to your breathing. As you breathe in, focus on filling your lungs slowly with air, then exhale to the count of **4**. As you exhale and the air flows out, notice how relaxing it feels as you come to number **4**.

- When you follow this routine five or six times you'll start to notice your neck and shoulders relax as you exhale. After the first week of daily practice, you may want to take even longer breaths to the count of **5** if you wish. Just decide what feels comfortable and helps you relax best.
- With daily practice, mindful breathing becomes second nature and very effective. That way you have the tension-reducing benefits whenever you need them. **Breathing exercises can help with any stressful situation**, not just exams.

You can enjoy the benefits of mindful breathing every day. Use it anytime you'd like to relax, reduce tension, improve your focus or get in the zone.

It helps to remain calm. Sometimes things just don't go smoothly. Stuff happens and you may not be as prepared as you'd like.

WIZARD'S TIP

Just Breathe. When you're facing an exam do your breathing exercises and relax. Focus on the now and do your best. If you've paid attention in class and worked with the Wizard's Guide you may surprise yourself.

Things To Remember

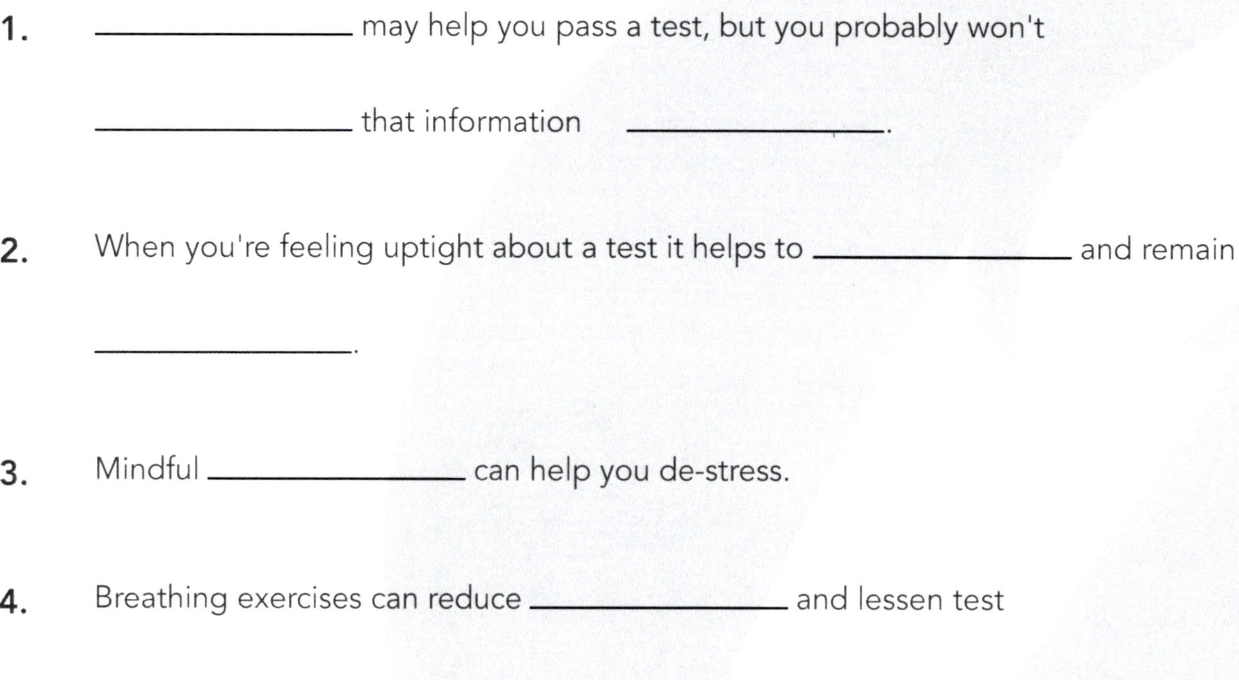

1. ________________ may help you pass a test, but you probably won't ________________ that information ________________.

2. When you're feeling uptight about a test it helps to ________________ and remain ________________.

3. Mindful ________________ can help you de-stress.

4. Breathing exercises can reduce ________________ and lessen test ________________.

Answer

1. Cramming remember later
2. breathe calm
3. breathing
4. stress anxiety

PREPARING FOR TESTS

In the learning lab scientists conduct research to find out what factors influence memory. Participants even stay overnight so researchers can study how sleep affects retention.

What helps memory work best? You'll be surprised but the answer is sleep and the timing of sleep. **The night before a test, going to bed right after you finish studying is essential.** In a study about the effects of sleep on learning **the group instructed to go directly to sleep after studying scored much higher** on a test the next morning. The group that was assigned to stay up and watch tv or play electronic games before going to bed scored much lower.

Wizard's Way

After reviewing the night before a test, you should go directly to sleep. No electronic gadgets, phones, computers, TV. Nothing, just straight to sleep. Doing that will ensure you'll remember what you'll need in order to do well.

TEST TYPES AND STRATEGIES

These are the main types of test formats you'll encounter:

- Short Answer Questions
- Fill in the Blank Questions
- Essay Questions
- Open Book and Take Home Tests
- Multiple Choice Questions

Teachers commonly use the first four.

Short Answer Questions generally ask for two to three sentence answers. They'll test your memory of facts or your ability to apply concepts you've learned.

Remember:

1. Pace yourself and don't rush.
2. Read the questions carefully. They can be tricky so pay attention.
3. Do the easiest questions first. Don't get stuck on any one question.
4. Write clear, legible answers.

Fill in the Blank Questions are straightforward and require that you remember specific information like facts or definitions. The answers are often based on class notes. In case you might have missed a class, be sure to borrow those notes from a classmate.

Essay Questions tend to be the most challenging. You need to read carefully, recall information and then formulate your answer in a well-organized paragraph. Simpler Essay Questions just want you to summarize facts or ideas. More challenging questions expect you to be creative and compare and contrast information, facts or concepts. **Be sure you really understand the question before you begin your answer.**

Handling Essay Questions

- Read each question carefully. Then formulate well-organized and complete answers.
- Decide on your approach. Jot down key points in an outline and follow it to stay on track.
- Time is essential. It's useful to answer the questions you're most confident about first.
- Be accurate and limit your answers to the specific questions.
- Present your answers logically and avoid listing random facts. "It's not a brain dump."
- Use complete sentences and write legibly.
- You can add supporting ideas later if time allows.
- Remember if you start to get stressed **just breathe.**

Wizard's Tip

Essay Questions are designed to test your understanding. Ask yourself, **"How do I know this?"** and **"Why is it important?".** Use your answers to frame your response and explain how new material relates to what you already know.

Working with Open Book and Take Home Tests

Open Book exams may seem like they should be a snap, but you can fall into a false sense of security. Before you know it, you've run out of time looking for answers. It's better to have a plan.

The first thing to remember is that you still need to study! As with all tests, preparation is key. Open Book tests ask you to demonstrate how well you understand the subject rather than how well you remember facts. Teachers expect you to consider the topic carefully and provide examples and brief quotes to support your answers.

Many Open Book tests are finals that cover a whole semester. You'll want to review the chapters again beforehand, especially the ones you haven't covered in a while.

Wizard's Tip

Many students use sticky notes to mark important pages. You can't highlight your textbook but **you can highlight key points in your notes.**

An Open Book test may be limited to only your textbook or to a specific set of notes. Your teacher will let you know beforehand what's allowed.

If open notes are permitted, take time to review and revise them. Get any notes you might have missed from a friend. Highlight key points, and prep formula sheets for math or science. Write down key phrases and dates. You know that word you always forget? Write it down! Prepare but don't try to anticipate the questions. This can lead you down the wrong path and waste time. It's also helpful to review the notes with a classmate.

For **Take Home Tests** you can use any materials on hand but remember, everything you need should be in either your textbook or notes. You're allowed more time on a Take Home Exam, so teachers expect well-written, structured answers. If you follow a plan you won't need to stay up all night. For essay questions, write from an outline. Be concise and keep your quotes short.

Plan your time wisely and answer what you know first. Don't leave questions blank if there's no penalty.

Remember it's only a test.
Prepare well and you'll do well.

Standardized Tests

Standardized Tests are achievement tests that assess general knowledge and skills. The tests are administered only to students in specific grades. These tests cover important required subjects such as English-Language Arts, Math or Science.

Standardized Tests are administered in a consistent, or "standard" way and are most often scored electronically.

Most Standardized Tests are made up of **Multiple Choice questions.** You'll read a selection followed by questions. Then you're required to select the most correct and complete answer from the available choices.

Dealing with Multiple Choice Questions

1. Time is always an important factor to consider, so pace yourself.
2. If you know the test time and the number of questions on that section, you can tell if you're keeping up. If you're behind, speed up a bit. If you're ahead, finish early so you can look over your answers.
3. Multiple Choice questions can be tricky. Stay calm and read each question very carefully.
4. Read all the answer choices. As soon as you recognize a correct answer, choose it and move right on.
5. Eliminate incorrect answers quickly to focus on alternatives.

6. If two of the four choices are obviously incorrect, continue right on to **decide which of the two remaining alternatives is correct**. That way it's more like answering a true/false question!

7. If you're unsure about an answer you may find a clue in one of the other questions.

8. If you've left any unanswered questions and you're certain there's no penalty for guessing, give it your best guess and go for it!

WIZARD'S TIP

If there's no penalty, never leave any Multiple Choice questions blank.

JUST FOR MATH

As we've said **Math is Special**. Math exams are a test of your problem-solving skills. If you've kept up on your work and asked for help when needed, you'll do fine.

There are still a few more things you need to remember about Math tests:

- Show your work. This will help keep you from getting lost and allow to you catch mistakes. Write as clearly as possible. **Remember: Teachers will often score partial credit even if you get the answer wrong as long as they see evidence you're on the right track.** They need to see the work!
- Keep all your work and don't erase a problem that you think may be incorrect. If you have time, review your work to help you zero in on any errors.
- Check for simple errors like a misplaced decimal point, or a missing negative sign, etc.

Wizard's Tip

Take time to memorize any formulas you'll need, then **write them out on scratch paper** at the start of the test. Writing them out will keep you focused and save you time. You'll be surprised.

This isn't "Rocket Science" — just breathe and think it through.

Things To Remember

1. When taking tests it's always important to read the questions ________________ and watch the ________________.

2. ________________ questions are the most challenging and designed to test your ________________.

3. Standardized achievement tests are often ________________ ________________.

4. On multiple choice questions, if there's no penalty for ________________ go for it!

Answer 

1. carefully time
2. Essay understanding
3. multiple choice
4. guessing

Painless Research Papers

CHAPTER 7

ORGANIZING YOUR PAPER

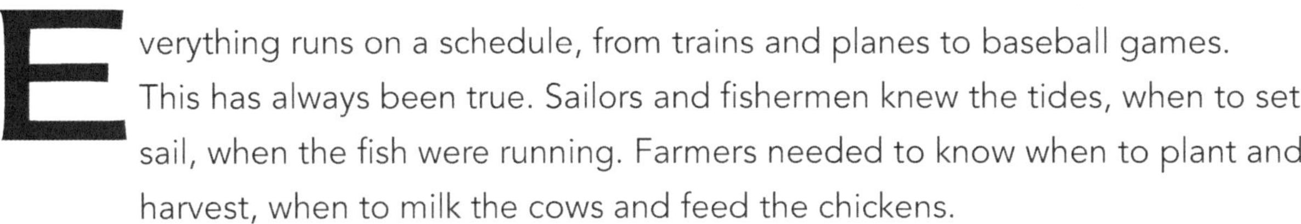

Everything runs on a schedule, from trains and planes to baseball games. This has always been true. Sailors and fishermen knew the tides, when to set sail, when the fish were running. Farmers needed to know when to plant and harvest, when to milk the cows and feed the chickens.

Today the world is more complex. Business people develop effective strategies that enable them to meet manufacturing deadlines, sourcing materials and parts from other companies all over the planet. Then they must successfully manufacture and deliver their products on time for their businesses to thrive.

Teachers customarily assign research papers weeks before they're due. Writing a paper not only challenges your research and writing abilities but also your planning skills. Your research paper is your product. When you put a logical plan into action with the right tools you'll do just fine.

Wizardry will ensure you deliver your best paper.

RESEARCH PAPER FRAMEWORK

Time Management is the key to success when writing research papers. Wizards know that using a structured approach delivers the best results. If your teacher doesn't assign a particular schedule, you won't go wrong using the **Wizard's Guide Research Paper Framework** as your roadmap. These time management guidelines will help keep you on track.

WIZARDS GUIDES® - Research Paper Framework

Name: ____________

Assignment Date: ________ **Due Date:** ________

Target Date for Completion: ________ O Done

Remember 4 days before due date!

1. If not assigned, Choose your topic by day 3 of the project: Date: ________ O Done

Topic: ____________

2. Gather Data:
   Start ________ Finish ________ O Done
3. Develop Outline:
   Start ________ Finish ________ O Done
4. First Draft:
   Start ________ Finish ________ O Done
5. Revision:
   Start ________ Finish ________ O Done
6. Final Draft:
   Start ________ Finish ________ O Done
7. Finished Copy:
   Start ________ Finish ________ O Done

Research Notes:

Irene Hartzell, PhD 2019© – downloads available at KidsLikeLearning.com/resources

Either way, you'll find useful ideas in the Wizard's Guide. The Research Paper Framework provides an easy to follow, step-by-step program. Use it to manage your time and resources, meet deadlines and deliver a paper you're proud of!

Defining Terms

Term Papers and Research Papers are often treated as the same thing, even viewed as synonymous, but they are actually different.

A Term Paper is designed to demonstrate understanding and mastery of essential skills and knowledge in a subject. A Term Paper can be a critical essay where you express your views on a topic. It can also be a research paper.

Term Papers are usually due near the end of the term and can account for a significant part of your grade.

Research Papers often require digging deeply into a subject using "research". Usually, you'll choose from topics related to the subject material you're studying. You may be required to select the topic or sometimes your teacher will give you a list to choose from.

Research Papers can have a central statement that your research seeks to support or explain. They can also have a question or a statement that you need to defend.

When given a choice, pick a topic that really interests you. Working on something you like will make a big difference in what you create and, ultimately, in your grade.

WRITING RESEARCH AND TERM PAPERS

Here are the usual steps Wizards follow when writing a simple Research Paper or Report:

1. Choose the Topic, if not assigned
2. Research and Gather Data
3. Develop the Outline
4. First Draft
5. Revision
6. Final Draft
7. Finished Copy

The Research Paper Framework is designed to keep you on target.

You're in charge of your schedule. Remember your teacher won't be assigning you daily homework for the paper.

You'll keep track of your due dates with the Framework and list everything you plan to do that week in the Weekly Assignment Matrix.

To start, you'll want to add the Research Paper tasks to the Wizard's Framework right away. The day the paper is assigned is when the clock starts ticking. You know when it's due, so write in:

- **The Assignment Date** (today's date)
- **The Due Date** (set by your teacher)
- The **Target Date for Completion** (4 days before the due date)

That way you know exactly how many days you have to work with.

That's the Wizard's Edge!

FOLLOW THE STEPS

Here we're using the example of a paper that's due in 3 weeks. That means the **Target Date for Completion** is in 17 days. Three weeks may seem like a lot of time, but it's not. So if you need to choose a Topic do so right away.

On DAY 1 select the Topic, if needed, and go ahead and fill out the rest of the Framework. **Add the exact dates you plan to start and finish every step.** Check them off when completed to stay on track.

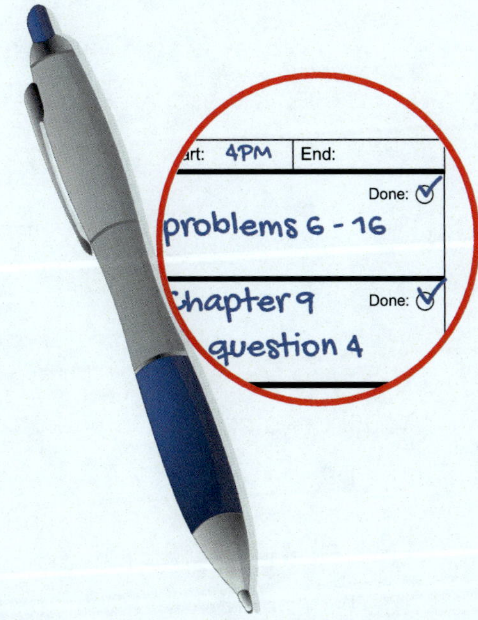

Note: This is only an example, so:
Remember to create your schedule based on the **actual time frame** of the assignment.

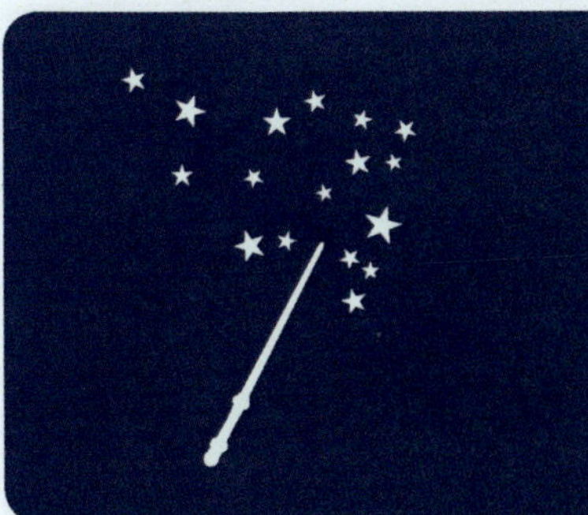

WIZARD'S TIP

It's easy to adjust your schedule if it's a long project. It's even more important to follow the Framework closely for shorter assignments.

1. **Choose the Topic** - DAY 1
If the Topic is already assigned, skip this step and use this extra day to begin the research and data gathering.

2. **Research & Gather Data** - DAYS 2 - 4
You'll start your research no later than DAY 2. **If the paper is due in 3 weeks, you can allow up to 3 days for this step.** Typically this step takes a fair amount of time. As you delve into the material you may find that you want to modify your topic. Maybe the Topic is too broad and you could be swamped with Data, or perhaps there's not enough.

The **Research Notes Matrix** (**Appendix A**) provides a systematic way to record the information that you find, your sources, keywords, notes, etc. Using the Matrix helps you stay organized.

Note: In Chapter 8 - The Wizard's Research Toolkit you'll find the latest tools to help make your job easier.

3. **Develop the Outline** - DAY 5
You'll develop the Outline on DAY 5. We'll talk about an easy strategy for outlining in a bit.

4. **First Draft** - DAYS 6 - 8
You'll begin the First Draft on DAY 6 and finish it no later than DAY 8. You have three days.

5. **Revision** - DAYS 9 - 11
Start no later than DAY 9, or as soon as you get feedback from your teacher. Your teacher will probably make some comments and suggestions on your Draft so follow them and make changes. You've allowed an extra day to revise the Draft.

6. **Final Draft** - DAYS 12 - 13
   Start on this no later than DAY 12 and complete and review the Final Draft in two days.

7. **Finished Copy** - DAYS 14 - 15
   Start the Finished Copy on DAY 14. You can allow up to two days.

Your tentative plan is to complete the project in 15 days which leaves two extra days, just in case.

Remember things can come up but that's ok, that's why Wizards use a Framework. You're covered and may even get done early! Sheer Magic!

WIZARD'S TIP

Wizards stay cool and collected because they have a plan. By sticking to your Framework you'll avoid that awful last minute rush.

CRAFTING YOUR PAPER

You've figured out the timing. The Framework provides a dependable structure so you can stay on schedule. It's time to work on the paper. You have the game plan now make it happen!

As you begin work on your Research Paper **remember to schedule tasks in the Weekly Assignment Matrix and add them to the Daily Study Matrix** the same as you do for all your other homework. You'll probably need to schedule at least one study period each day for your project.

WIZARD'S WAY

Setting and meeting your Target Dates keeps you on track to deliver your best possible paper on time!

Tips to handle each step

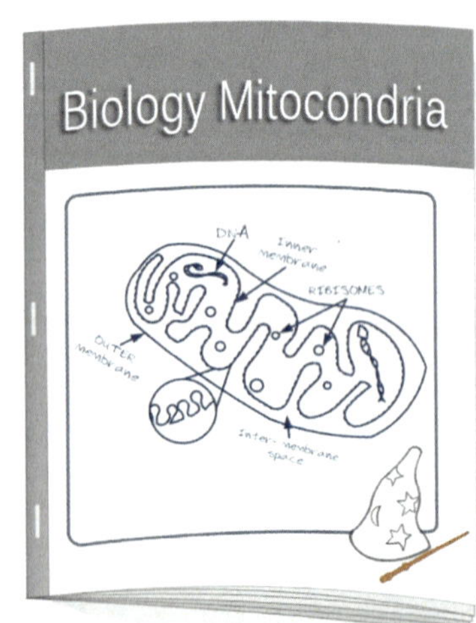

1. **Choose the Topic**
   If you don't have assigned Topics, try to pick yours on DAY 1. Follow your teacher's guidelines and you won't go wrong. You can always refine it as you go along.

   Choosing a Topic is a crucial step that guides the development of your entire project. Research papers are an opportunity to dive into a topic that really interests you.

If you have trouble deciding on your focus, why not set up one of the Daily Study Matrix 40 minute study periods to brainstorm? Think about the Topic, look over your preliminary research and jot down your main interests. See how they fit together. Is there a chronological order or other pattern?

Ask: Can this Topic be covered in the time limits and within the guidelines? If the Topic is too narrow, you might not find sufficient information to write about. You'll need to choose a broader Topic. You can also become very enthusiastic about a particular subject with overwhelming mountains of information. But don't worry, it's usually easier to narrow the scope of your Topic than to expand it. After your initial research don't hesitate to focus on the parts that interest you. Keep to the guidelines but be flexible.

WIZARD'S TIP

If you find it's difficult to decide on a Topic talk with your teacher for guidance. Selecting a Topic that excites you will help you get the job done well.

2. **Research and Gather Data**
   This step typically takes the most time. Use the **Wizard's Research Notes to organize your data** and keep track of sources.

   If your teacher provides resources and guidelines for your research, start with those. **The Wizard's Research Toolkit - Chapter 8** covers useful tools and strategies to aid in your research.

3. **Develop the Outline**
Look over what you've found and think about the main topics and concepts.

- Write each one down on a separate index card.
- Arrange the cards in a logical sequence to help decide on headings for the Outline.
- After you finish check to be sure the cards are complete and create the Outline.

Having a well-organized, detailed Outline will make writing the First Draft a snap.

4. **First Draft**
Now you'll proceed to write the First Draft using the Outline as a framework. You may decide to budget some extra time for this step, just in case you need to do more research.

Ask a friend or family member to read over the First Draft for feedback to be certain your ideas are clear and complete. Suggestions you receive may be very helpful.

As you write up the First Draft, be sure to check that it will meet the length requirements. If the paper is too short, or even too long you may lose points.

5. **The Revision Process**
If you receive feedback from your teacher on the First Draft, make the corrections, and use the time to polish and improve your paper. It's an opportunity to review what you've written, and be sure you haven't omitted anything important. Check to see that it flows smoothly.

Also, review the spelling and punctuation. Spell Check can seem like magic, but Wizards know that sometimes it can change words in unintended ways so check it over yourself!

Avoid overly long and run-on sentences. If a section doesn't flow right a useful technique is to read it aloud or have someone else read that part to you. When you "hear" it, you'll catch stuff you may have missed or left out, you'll hear things that sound wrong. Those are spots where you might want to word things differently. This really helps.

6. **Final Draft**

When you're satisfied with the Revision write the Final Draft. Ask another friend to read the paper and critique it one last time. This may be your final opportunity to modify and correct the content or improve the flow of ideas.

7. **Finished Copy**

Prepare the Finished Copy so it's complete four days before it's due. Take a last look at writing style, neatness and for any typos.

Things To Remember

1. Using the Wizard's Guide ________________ ________________ Framework will help you complete your paper on time.

2. ________________ Management is the key to a successful paper.

3. The day the research paper is assigned you'll set a Target Date for ________________ to finish the paper 4 days before it's due.

4. Then you'll set ________________ dates to ________________ each step.

Answer 

1. Research Paper
2. Time
3. completion
4. specific complete

PRESENTING YOUR PAPER

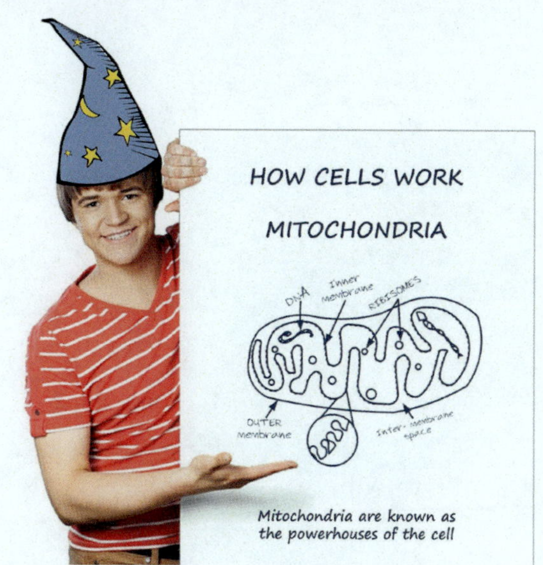

Often you'll be required to present your paper to the class. Wizards know that conveying information effectively and speaking to a group is a very valuable life skill.

You'll be surprised how often in life you'll be expected to speak before a group. **Being comfortable as a presenter may be one of the most important skills you'll ever gain.**

Here are a few pointers:

- Make eye contact with your listeners, maintaining good eye contact encourages interest.
- Good posture helps you focus and your audience will pay more attention to what you have to say, so be relaxed but don't slouch.
- We've already suggested speaking up in class, so raising your hand and asking or answering questions is good practice. Becoming accustomed to speaking in front of people is another benefit of class participation.
- Presentations are often interactive and listeners will expect to be able to ask questions. Before giving a presentation, step back and read through your paper and consider what questions might naturally arise. If you anticipate questions it becomes easier to answer them. That also helps your confidence. If you find there's an important point you haven't covered, consider adding it to your report if there's time.
- When responding to questions try to avoid just giving one or two word answers. That can tend to shut down communication. Using complete sentences works better.

- You can also rehearse your presentation in front of a mirror to evaluate your body language. Another option is to record yourself with your phone and play it back to see how you sound.
- Stay aware of time and think about the key points you plan to make in the time you have. This is called pacing. If you can, practice with a timer to get your pacing down. You can also give your talk to a friend or even a small group. Practice makes you a more confident speaker.
- If you will be presenting as part of a group decide who will say what and practice handing off to each other. Again, everyone needs to be aware of timing.
- If you use PowerPoint remember to only include the key points you want to talk about, along with supporting material (graphs, charts and pictures) to illustrate those points. You'll do the same thing if you're presenting from a flip board or writing out your points on the whiteboard.
- The fonts in a PowerPoint presentation should be 30 points or larger. Remember your presentation needs to be readable from across the room.

Wizard's Tip

Know your equipment! Technical problems can really throw you off. If you're using a laptop and projector, test it out beforehand "several times" and make sure everything is working the way it should.

Wizard's Way

Wizards know that good preparation is one of the best ways to prevent stage fright.

Prepare and remember to breathe; you'll do fine.

Things To Remember

1. Being able to speak to a group is a very ______________ life ______________.

2. Maintaining good ______________ contact with your audience encourages ______________.

3. Use bullet points, include the ______________ points you're talking about.

4. Along with supporting ______________ to illustrate those points.

5. Technical problems can throw you off. Test your ______________ "several times" beforehand.

1. valuable skill
2. eye interest
3. key
4. material
5. equipment

Wizard's Research Toolkit

CHAPTER 8

GETTING THE JOB DONE

Once you have a topic for the paper, it's time to begin your research and data gathering. This used to be much harder but even with search engines it still can take a lot of time. After you've picked your topic and narrowed your focus, understanding what tools are out there and how to use them is your first step to a brilliant paper. Here's the **Wizard's Research Toolkit** with the tools you'll need:

GOOGLE SEARCH

It's probably simplest if you begin your research with **Google**. You may already be a Wizard at that but here are some helpful tips:

Google was developed (by Wizards) to make it easy for people to find information and it works extremely well. Google search is easy to use, but Wizards know ways to make Google work even better.

http://

Search operators — These are characters that you can type in to tell Google how and what you want it to search for.

Three of the main search operators are:

1. **Quotation Marks** ("") If you put quotes around your search that tells Google to search only for the exact phrase.

2. **Plus Sign**(+) It lets you combine things. It works like the word "and". For example, if you entered "tortoise + hippo" in the search box you would find articles about a baby hippopotamus orphaned by the tsunami in 2012 that was adopted by a giant tortoise (a true story) instead of random items about tortoises and hippos.

3. **Minus Sign** (-) means not, so if you want information about the planet Saturn and not Saturn the car you would type "Saturn-car"

You can use search operators in the Google search box, but Google also has an advanced search page. Just add **/advanced_search** to google.com, https://google.com/advanced_search

The form offers you a way to fine-tune your search and the search operators are explained on the left.

Google

Advanced Search

Find pages with...		To do this in the search box
all these words:		Type the important words: tricolor rat terrier
this exact phrase:		Put exact words in quotes: "rat terrier"
any of these words:		Type ORbetween all the words you want: miniature ORstandard
none of these words:		Put a minus sign just before words you don't know -rodent, -"Jack Russel"
Numbers ranging from:	to	Put to periods between the numbers and add a unit of measure 10..35 16, $300..$500

Then narrow your search by:		
language:	▾	Find pages in the language you select.
region:	▾	Find pages published in a particular region.
last update:	▾	Find pages updated within the last month.
site or domain:	▾	Search one site (like Wikipedia.org) or limit your search to a domain name like .edu, .org or .gov
terms appearing:	▾	Search for terms in the whole page, page title or web address or links to the page you're looking for.
Safe Search	▾	Tell Safe Search whether to view sexually explicit content.
file type:	▾	Find pages in the format you prefer.
usage rights:	▾	Find pages you are free to use yourself.

Advanced Search

Fun Fact: Using Google's search operators to find what you want is a type of Math called **Boolean Algebra** that calculates with **true** and **false** values instead of numbers. It has three basic operators **and, or** and **not**. They compare: this **and** that, this **not** that, and this **or** that — it's a type of math or logic that you use all the time but don't even think about. It's named after **George Boole** a 19th-century mathematician who helped lay the foundation for modern computer science.

OTHER GOOGLE TOOLS

Wizards also take advantage of other Google services including:

Google Scholar - searches research papers

https://scholar.google.com/ Google Scholar now allows you to save your searches in a library, set up alerts for your research and even has a special tool to help with citations.

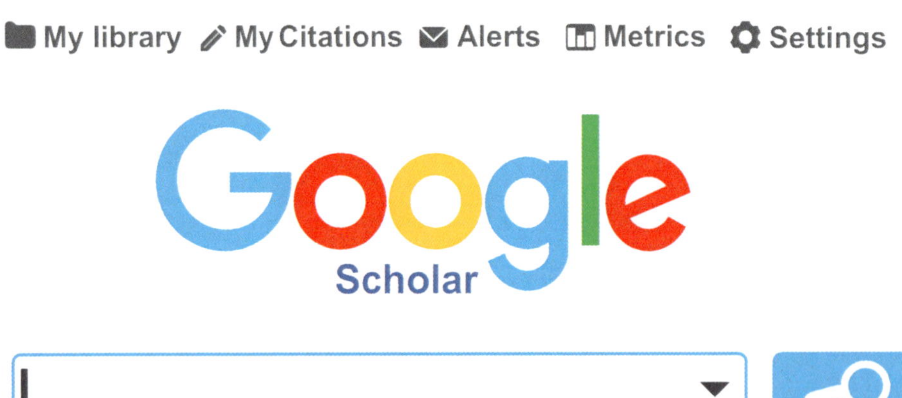

Stand on the shoulders of giants

Google Books - helps you find books you can get from the library https://books.google.com/

Google Translate - allows you to read text translation from over a hundred languages https://translate.google.com/

Many older books are in the public domain, that means they are freely available. Many can now be read in full online. Other important resources include online libraries such as:

Project Gutenberg https://www.gutenberg.org/

Library of Congress https://www.loc.gov/

Google Maps & Google Earth

Google Maps is a fascinating tool, especially when you understand what you can do with it. Let's look at Perth, a modern city in Australia. It has the distinction of being the most isolated big city in the world. Perth, on the sparsely populated south west coast of Australia, is further away from other population centers than any metropolitan area on earth. The closest comparable city is Adelaide 2136 kilometers (1327 miles) away.

It takes a minimum of two days and at least three plane changes to fly there from the U.S. By using **Google Maps** and **Google Earth**, you can explore the whole city and virtually drive down each street from your computer. You can do the same with just about any big city anywhere in the world. It gets even better. More and more interesting places from museums to historical points of interest are getting virtual walk throughs. You can view the paintings in a museum, tour the great pyramids in Egypt, or explore caverns underground. Even fictional places are getting this treatment. You can tour Diagon Alley, or if you find the right police box in London, visit Dr Who's TARDIS.

You can even bend time. For example, we humans have been taking photos for over 150 years. More and more of these images have been indexed, located and linked to Google Earth. Now many locations will even let you peek into the past. We have a list of interesting walk-throughs on https://KidsLikeLearning/Guides

Google Earth even includes the Moon, Oceans, 3D tours of famous buildings and historical images that take you back in time.

- With **Google Mars**, you can fly through Mariner Valley or follow along where our robots have gone exploring. https://www.google.com/mars/

- **Google Sky** lets you explore the rest of the universe. https://www.google.com/sky/

Now that's magic!

There's lots more to learn about how to use Google, but we'll leave that for you to explore. Here's a really useful link that'll help guide your Google searches: https://support.google.com/websearch

So, using a Search Engine, you'll take notes and begin gathering material. You'll also want to look for further information directly from books and articles. Your teacher or a librarian can provide suggestions about additional sources and even specific websites.

Don't forget to record your notes and sources using the **Wizard's Research Notes** form so you can keep them in one, easy-to-find place. (see Appendix A)

OTHER RESOURCES

Wikipedia

By Middle School, most students are familiar with **Wikipedia**. You probably have some idea of what it's about. Many people are concerned with Wikipedia's accuracy because anyone is allowed to edit it. Except with some areas of current events and politics, Wikipedia seems to be very accurate. In fact studies show, the error rate is actually lower than that of the **Encyclopedia Britannica**.

Many teachers tend to actively discourage students from relying only on Wikipedia. There are good reasons for that, not the least of which is that it's not a good idea to rely too heavily on any single source of information. Even if your teacher limits the number of Wikipedia citations or won't allow them at all, it's still a great jumping off place to start your research.

You can even become an editor on Wikipedia. Here's the link:
https://en.wikipedia.org/wiki/Wikipedia:Introduction

Libraries and Library Websites

If you find you need a book, you can check their catalog online and save yourself a trip. You can see if they have it, whether it's available and even put a hold on the book. You might find just what you're looking for as a downloadable eBook too. eBooks can even be checked out if the library is closed. You may also be able to log in from home to specialized news services and databases through your library's website.

Wizard's Tip

Librarians are Wizards! If you get stuck, ask a librarian. They'll be able to point you in the right direction and probably direct you to resources that you've never even considered.

Conducting interviews can be a very interesting way to research a subject. Depending on the topic you may be able to interview people with firsthand knowledge or experience. Veterans, doctors, professionals, artists, and seniors are just a sample of the types of people you could ask to participate.

Scholastic has a helpful article on interviewing techniques here: http://www.scholastic.com/teachers/article/how-conduct-journalistic-interview

Wizard's Way

Wizards know **interviewing** is a life skill to cultivate. There's a knack to talking to people and asking just the right questions. **Take the time to develop it.** You'll be surprised how useful it becomes.

News, Magazines and Documentaries

We live in a world surrounded by news and opinion. You may decide to use a topic in the day's **news** as the jumping off point for an assignment. Since much of the TV and radio news consists of 15 - 30 second sound bytes, brief newspaper articles or short blog posts, you'll probably need to dig deeper to find what you need.

You can find more in-depth information and reporting in magazines, journals or documentaries. Many of these sources can be found online. Sometimes you can even get subscription publications via a library's website using your card number.

Your librarian can help!

TECHNOLOGY & AI

As always, Technology is changing!

One important recent development has been the advent of **AI's** wanting to talk with you. Voice interactivity is a big trend. Today we interact with computers via keyboard, mouse, touchscreen, etc. A major shift has happened and voice interactivity is the new reality.

Programs like **Siri, Alexa** and other **Artificially Intelligent Agents** will become the main way we interact with information online. That's why we're including AI in the Guide.

People have been talking about Artificial Intelligence and smart robots for a long time, you've probably seen the movies. So an important thing to understand is what is real and what's fiction, what AI is and what it isn't.

These agents or bots are just software programs based on **learning algorithms**. And up to a point, these algorithms allow them to become better at what they can do. IBM's Deep Blue learned how to beat the world's top chess masters way back in 1996.

They're great at solving certain types of problems, especially involving lots of data. With advances in our understanding of Language, Vision, Genetics, and Medical Diagnostics, combined with Simulation and Modeling, AI will change the world.

Virtual Assistants & Voice Interface

Our real question is: How can a Wizard best make use of them? All these programs, Apple's Siri, Amazon's Alexa, Microsoft's Cortana or Google's Assistant offer powerful tools to help you find information. They excel in finding specific facts, and this can be very helpful when working on an assignment.

For example, ask Alexa, "what's the highest peak in California" and it will name the mountain and give you some useful specifics. You may need to ask a couple of questions to find everything you want, but it's generally faster than typing your search because these programs understand English.

What they can do goes beyond answering questions. You can also use these tools to set timers and reminders. They can even integrate with your calendar, and help you stay on track. To make the best use of software agents it's important that you **speak clearly and ask specific questions.**

If you don't have one of these tools on your phone, you can explore voice commands with Google's search assistant in Chrome. When you open up Google Search in the Chrome browser, you may have noticed a little microphone inside the search window. If you click on it, you can ask a question.

You will need to use a microphone with your computer of course, but most laptops have them built in. If you ask, 'what is the tallest peak in California?' it will come back with a reply listing several of the tallest peaks, their height and other information. It will also bring up relevant pages below the search field. **These are exactly the same results you'd get if you typed in the query.**

You need to speak clearly and enunciate. The more specific your question is, the better.

Google has been developing something called **Semantic Search** that understands natural language so voice search is only going to become easier to use. Every time someone interacts with it, it learns more. Soon you'll be able to speak directly to Google and ask questions as if you were talking to a person, which will save you lots of time.

Voice interaction is still very new and is becoming more sophisticated as time goes on. So for now, use it for specific questions. But do keep an eye on it and watch for new capabilities, so you'll stay ahead of the game.

We'll be updating this topic at http://kidslikelearning.com/Guides as the tools develop and capabilities expand.

Type with your voice in Google Docs

Google Docs is another tool with a voice interactivity option. To try it, you'll need a **Google account**. Login and open up Google Docs in the **Chrome browser** — You can find it by clicking on the Google Apps Icon (grid of nine boxes) to the right hand-side of the search window inside Gmail.

Many of you already use Google Docs for class. In fact, Docs is the main tool we've used to collaborate in creating this book.

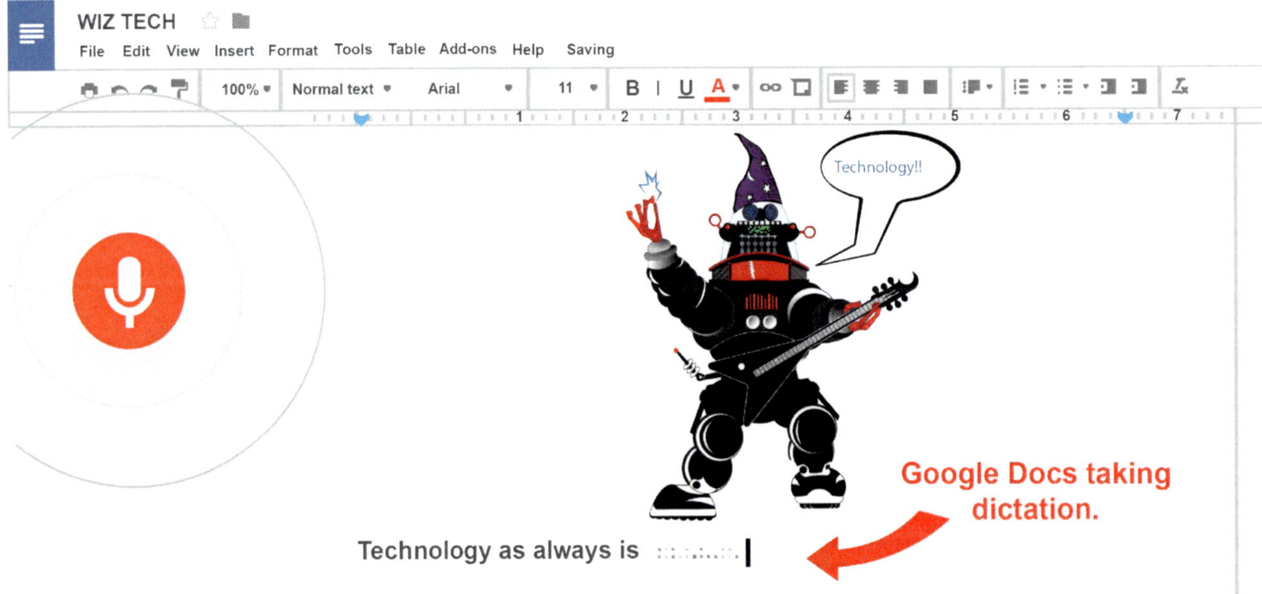

What you may not already know is that you can compose and edit documents by speaking directly to Google Docs.

It's already available and like Chrome's voice search, all you need is a microphone. Then you can use Voice Recognition to write. Not only will it transcribe your words but Docs recognizes commands to add punctuation and formatting to your document.

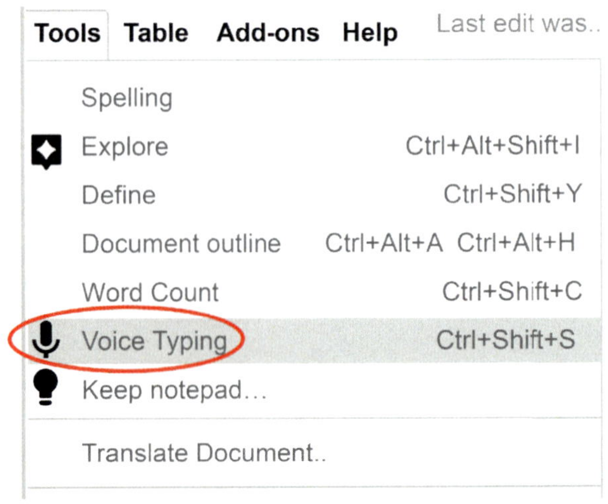

It's a useful tool to explore and it can be very helpful getting your initial ideas down. You can find it under the drop-down for Tools.

Scroll over the microphone icon on the left side of the screen then click on the little question mark. It provides complete instructions on how to use the voice commands. It's fun and as you explore, you'll probably find many ways to make good use of it.

Things to know:
First, as with voice search, you must speak clearly — second **proofread!** Voice recognition isn't perfect yet. You don't want to turn in a paper with "Yucatan cheese" instead of "you can choose". Google Docs can be found at https://docs.google.com

Virtual & Augmented Reality

VR and AR, more acronyms to pay attention to!

These technologies will allow you to interact with objects in a 3d virtual space (VR) or overlaid right onto your classroom (AR). It's similar to how we interact with Google Earth. Imagine exploring a cell from the inside, or working on a project together with kids in another school as if they were right there in you.

Many companies are already developing this technology. For example, Microsoft's AR HoloLens is already available and used in schools now for teaching science and math.

Wizards are explorers, dive in and check it out.

WIZARD'S TIP

Wizards want you to ask questions, and we give you the tools to find answers. Use them, research, and think about what you can do to have the life you want. **Remember Anything is possible!**

Throughout **A Wizard's Guide** we've talked about "Research" and tested methods that we know work. Some of you may be curious about this, so we've added a link to a Special Page on **Kids Like Learning**. There we gathered links to papers published in scientific journals, as well as articles from magazines like **Scientific American** or **NewsWeek** designed to explain the research in plain language. We also plan to update this list as new research comes to our attention, and to add new tips as Wizards around the world invent new ways of making things work.

Explore!

If you have a Tip to share with other wizards, let us know at the link below and we may publish it on our blog. Look for http//KidsLikeLearning.com/Guides under Research.

Downloadables

APPENDIX A

WIZARD'S MATRIX FORMS

- Weekly Assignment Matrix - part A
- Weekly Assignment Matrix - part B
- Weekly Assignment Matrix - part A - Alternate Note: You can use this form to have facing pages and view the week at a glance. It's set up to be hole punched on the right hand side.
- Daily Study Matrix
- Wizard's Guide - Research Paper Framework
- Wizard's Research Notes
- Wizard's Notes

The printable worksheets of the Wizard's Matrix can be found on the following pages.

WIZARDS GUIDES®

WEEKLY ASSIGNMENT MATRIX

Name: ______________________

Week of: ______________________

Subjects

MON	TUE	WED

STUDY ALERTS!

Hole punch this side for facing pages.

WIZARDS GUIDES®

WEEKLY ASSIGNMENT MATRIX

Name: ______________________

Week of: ______________________

Subjects	THU	FRI	WEEK END

STUDY ALERTS!

WIZARDS GUIDES®

WEEKLY ASSIGNMENT MATRIX

Name: ______________________

Week of: ______________________

Subjects	MON	TUE	WED

STUDY ALERTS!

WIZARDS GUIDES® - Daily Study Matrix

Name: ____________________ Date: ____________________

CIRCLE THE DAY MON TUE WED THU FRI SAT SUN

Start:	End:

#	SUBJECT:	START:	Done:
1			○
2			○
3			○
4			○
5			○
6			○
7			○
8			○
9			○

NOTES

Make a Habit of Lifelong Learning

Irene Hartzell, PhD **2019** **– downloads available at KidsLikeLearning.com/resources**

WIZARDS GUIDES® - Research Paper Framework

Name: ____________________

Assignment Date: ____________ **Due Date:** ____________

Target Date for Completion: ____________ O Done

Remember 4 days before due date!

1. If not assigned, Choose your topic by day 3 of the project: Date: ____________

O Done

Topic: ______________________________________

2. Gather Data:

Start ____________ Finish ____________ O Done

3. Develop Outline:

Start ____________ Finish ____________ O Done

4. First Draft:

Start ____________ Finish ____________ O Done

5. Revision:

Start ____________ Finish ____________ O Done

6. Final Draft:

Start ____________ Finish ____________ O Done

7. Finished Copy:

Start ____________ Finish ____________ O Done

Research Notes:

____

____

____

____

____

____

WIZARDS GUIDES® - Wizard's Research Notes

Name:

Topic: ______________________ Due Date: __________

Outline: __________ First Draft: __________ Final Draft: __________

Sources:

Summary:

Key Points:	Notes:

WIZARDS GUIDES®

Wizard's Notes

Name:

Summary:

Key Points:	Notes:

Summary:

Key Points:	Notes:

Reading Speed

APPENDIX B

PRACTICE

Alice in Wonderland was first published in 1865 as **Alice's Adventures in Wonderland** by Lewis Carroll with illustrations by John Tenniel.

We are using "Alice" for several reasons:

1. After more than a hundred and fifty years it's in the Public Domain, which means that anyone is free to make use of it.

2. Even though it was written in the mid 19th century the language is surprisingly readable for people today.

3. And **it's just plain fun!**

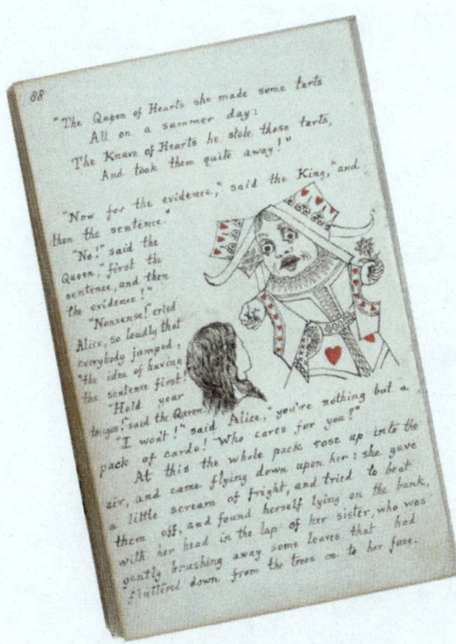

88

"The Queen of Hearts she made some tarts
All on a summer day:
The Knave of Hearts he stole those tarts,
And took them quite away!"

"Now for the evidence," said the King, "and then the sentence."

"No!" said the Queen, "first the sentence, and then the evidence!"

"Nonsense!" cried Alice, so loudly that everybody jumped, "the idea of having the sentence first!"

"Hold your tongue!" said the Queen.

"I won't!" said Alice, "you're nothing but a pack of cards! Who cares for you?"

At this the whole pack rose up into the air, and came flying down upon her: she gave a little scream of fright, and tried to beat them off, and found herself lying on the bank, with her head in the lap of her sister, who was gently brushing away some leaves that had fluttered down from the trees on to her face.

We've included chapter one of Alice in Wonderland, highlighted in groups of two words, then in three. The highlighting is to help you get used to seeing the words in groups

We highlighted every two or three words in chapter 1 regardless of sense. You may notice that after a while you'll start grouping the words differently as your brain will start interpreting the words unconsciously in ways that do make sense, ways that form a clear thought.

For example we grouped every three words like this:

Alice was not a bit hurt, and she jumped up in a moment. She looked up, but it was all dark overhead; before her was another long passage and the White Rabbit was still in sight, hurrying down it. There was not a moment to be lost. Away went Alice like the wind and was just in time to hear it say, as it turned a corner, 'Oh, my ears and whiskers, how late it's getting!' She was close behind it when she turned the corner, but the Rabbit was no longer to be seen.

But after practice you might group them differently, like:

Alice was not a bit hurt, and she jumped up in a moment. She looked up, but it was all dark overhead; before her was another long passage and the White Rabbit was still in sight, hurrying down it. There was not a moment to be lost. Away went Alice like the wind and was just in time to hear it say, as it turned a corner, 'Oh, my ears and whiskers, how late it's getting!' She was close behind it when she turned the corner, but the Rabbit was no longer to be seen.

If that happens, don't worry about it **and don't try to force yourself to read only three words**, It's just your brain doing its job and making sense of the patterns. You're getting into the the flow.

Just Breathe, you're in the Zone!

Reading Selection from

ALICE'S ADVENTURES IN WONDERLAND

1.DOWN THE RABBIT-HOLE

Alice was beginning to get very tired of sitting by her sister on the bank, and of having nothing to do. Once or twice she had peeped into the book her sister was reading, but it had no pictures or conversations in it, 'and what is the use of a book,' thought Alice, 'without pictures or conversations?

So she was considering in her own mind (as well as she could, for the day made her feel very sleepy and stupid), whether the pleasure of making a daisy-chain would be worth the trouble of getting up and picking the daisies, when suddenly a White Rabbit with pink eyes ran close by her.

There was nothing so very remarkable in that, nor did Alice think it so very much out of the way to hear the Rabbit say to itself, 'Oh dear! Oh dear! I shall be too late!' But when the Rabbit actually took a watch out of its waistcoat-pocket and looked at it and then hurried on, Alice started to her feet, for it flashed across her mind that she had never before seen a rabbit with either a waistcoat-pocket, or a watch to take out of it, and, burning with curiosity, she ran across the field after it and was just in time to see it pop down a large rabbit-hole, under the hedge. In another moment, down went Alice after it!

The rabbit-hole went straight on like a tunnel for some way and then dipped suddenly down, so suddenly that Alice had not a moment to think about stopping herself before she found herself falling down what seemed to be a very deep well.

Either the well was very deep, or she fell very slowly, for she had plenty of time, as she went down, to look about her. First, she tried to make out what she was coming to, but it was too dark to see anything; then she looked at the sides of the well and noticed that they were filled with cupboards and book-shelves; here and there she saw maps and pictures hung upon pegs. She took down a jar from one of the shelves as she passed. It was labeled "ORANGE MARMALADE," but, to her great disappointment, it was empty; she did not like to drop the jar, so managed to put it into one of the cupboards as she fell past it.

Down, down, down! Would the fall never come to an end? There was nothing else to do, so Alice soon began talking to herself. "Dinah'll miss me very much to-night, I should think!" (Dinah was the cat.) "I hope they'll remember her saucer of milk at tea-time. Dinah, my dear, I wish you were down here with me!" Alice felt that she was dozing off, when suddenly, thump! thump! down she came upon a heap of sticks and dry leaves, and the fall was over.

Now three words at a time

Alice was not a bit hurt, and she jumped up in a moment. She looked up, but it was all dark overhead; before her was another long passage and the White Rabbit was still in sight, hurrying down it. There was not a moment to be lost. Away went Alice like the wind and was just in time to hear it say, as it turned a corner, "Oh, my ears and whiskers, how late it's getting!" She was close behind it when she turned the corner, but the Rabbit was no longer to be seen.

She found herself in a long, low hall, which was lit up by a row of lamps hanging from the roof. There were doors all 'round the hall, but they were all locked; and when Alice had been all the way down one side and up the other, trying every door, she walked sadly down the middle, wondering how she was ever to get out again.

Suddenly she came upon a little table, all made of solid glass. There was nothing on it but a tiny golden key, and Alice's first idea was that this might belong to one of the doors of the hall; but, alas! either the locks were too large, or the key was too small but, at any rate, it would not open any of them. However, on the second time 'round, she came upon a low curtain she had not noticed before, and behind it was a little door about fifteen inches high. She tried the little golden key in the lock, and to her great delight, it fitted!

Alice opened the door and found that it led into a small passage, not much larger than a rat-hole; she knelt down and looked along the passage into the loveliest garden you ever saw. How she longed to get out of that dark hall and wander about among those beds of bright flowers and those cool fountains, but she could not even get her head through the doorway. "Oh," said Alice, "how I wish I could shut up like a telescope! I think I could, if I only knew how to begin."

Alice went back to the table, half hoping she might find another key on it, or at any rate, a book of rules for shutting people up like telescopes. This time she found a little bottle on it ('which certainly was not here before,' said Alice), and tied 'round the neck of the bottle was a paper label, with the words "DRINK ME" beautifully printed on it in large letters.

" No, I'll look first," she said, "and see whether it's marked 'poison' or not," for she had never forgotten that, if you drink from a bottle marked 'poison', it is almost certain to disagree with you, sooner or later. However, this bottle was not marked 'poison', so Alice ventured to taste it, and, finding it very nice (it had a sort of mixed flavor of cherry-tart, custard, pineapple, roast turkey, toffee and hot buttered toast), she very soon finished it off.

"What a curious feeling!" said Alice. "I must be shutting up like a telescope!"

And so it was indeed! She was now only ten inches high, and her face brightened up at the thought that she was now the right size for going through the little door into that lovely garden.

After a while, finding that nothing more happened, she decided on going into the garden at once; but, alas for poor Alice!
When she got to the door, she found she had forgotten the little golden key, and when she went back to the table for it, she found she could not possibly reach it: she could see it quite plainly through the glass and she tried her best to climb up one of the legs of the table, but it was too slippery, and when she had tired herself out with trying, the poor little thing sat down and cried.

"Come, there's no use in crying like that!" said Alice to herself rather sharply. "I advise you to leave off this minute!" She generally gave herself very good advice (though she very seldom followed it), and sometimes she scolded herself so severely as to bring tears into her eyes.

Soon her eye fell on a little glass box that was lying under the table: she opened it and found in it a very small cake, on which the words "EAT ME" were beautifully marked in currants. "Well, I'll eat it," said Alice, "and if it makes me grow larger, I can reach the key; and if it makes me grow smaller, I can creep under the door: so either way I'll get into the garden, and I don't care which happens!"

She ate a little bit and said anxiously to herself, "Which way? Which way?" holding her hand on the top of her head to feel which way she was growing; and she was quite surprised to find that she remained the same size. So she set to work and very soon finished off the cake.

Note: Alice's Adventures in Wonderland is available in its entirety through project Gutenberg at https://www.gutenberg.org/ebooks/19033

If you are interested in Alice, who was a real person you can find out more on Wikipedia: https://en.wikipedia.org/wiki/Alice's_Adventures_in_Wonderland

AUTHOR BIO

Irene J. Hartzell, Ph.D. has three decades of experience in psychology and education. She's credentialed as a teacher, counselor and school psychologist. She began her studies as a Psychology major at Reed College. Then she completed the Vor Diplom Pruefung at LudwigMaximiians-Universit't in Munich, Germany. While at LMU Munich Irene's perspectives on education were opened to a much broader range of possibilities.

She received a Bachelor's degree in Psychology and a Master's degree in Education from the University of California Berkeley. Her Ph.D. in Counseling Psychology was awarded at the University of Oregon where she was a U.S. Vocational Rehabilitation Administration Fellow.

Having personally overcome ADHD and developed strategies on her own to achieve academic success, Dr. Hartzell is very familiar with the challenges K-12 students face. Her background uniquely qualifies her to help them understand what's needed in order to do well and succeed in the classroom.

A Wizard's Guide to Study Skills is her latest, most important contribution. Techniques based on human learning research and classroom proven strategies give students the "know how" to become academic Wizards.

A Wizard's Guide teaches the "essential job skills" needed by students in today's classrooms. Mastering these skills makes studying flow better so homework doesn't drag on. With simple ways to increase their reading speed and prepare for tests, kids gain new confidence. As students use their new skills and begin to achieve greater academic success they regain their natural joy in learning.

A Wizard's Guide would not have happened without the help, patience and support of librarians and Libraries in Washington and California.

- The Seattle Public Library's Central Library, Seattle WA
- Los Gatos Library, Los Gatos CA
- Sunnyvale Public Library, Sunnyvale CA
- Santa Clara Central Park Library, Santa Clara CA
- Dr. Martin Luther King Jr. Library, San Jose CA

Remember, Librarians are all Wizards!

Thank You All for your help and support throughout this project.

Made in the USA
Middletown, DE
03 April 2023

28147719R10071